First published in Great Britain in 2022 by Wren & Rook

ISBN: 978 1 5263 6441 8
E-book ISBN: 978 1 5263 6442 5

10 9 8 7 6 5 4 3 2 1

MIX
Paper from
responsible sources
FSC
www.fsc.org   FSC® C104740

Wren & Rook
An imprint of
Hachette Children's Group
Part of Hodder & Stoughton
Carmelite House
50 Victoria Embankment
London EC4Y 0DZ

An Hachette UK Company
www.hachette.co.uk
www.hachettechildrens.co.uk

Printed and bound in Great Britain by Clays Ltd, Elcograf S.p.A

ONJALI Q. RAÚF

Hope on the Horizon

A CHILDREN'S HANDBOOK ON EMPATHY, KINDNESS & MAKING A BETTER WORLD

ILLUSTRATED BY ISOBEL LUNDIE
COVER ILLUSTRATION
BY PIPPA CURNICK

wren & rook

For anyone who has ever had
a kind thought and acted on it,
and all the sparks of hope that
keep this world turning.

CONTENTS

A little note to my lovely readers

Before we get started on this adventure together, it's important for you to know that I will occasionally be highlighting some incredibly difficult issues which exist in our world — issues which I wish didn't exist, but which sadly do.

If you find yourself, at any moment, becoming upset or anxious over anything I write about, please don't hesitate to ask your most favourite and trusted grown-up — be they at home or at school — any questions you may have.

Or if you don't want to do that, skip the paragraph(s) completely, and start on another. No one will know, and even if someone did run right over to tell me, I wouldn't mind in the slightest! (In fact, I would give you a personal round of applause and a big hug for skipping over the bits you aren't quite ready for.)

If you, or someone you love, is also experiencing something I highlight, please turn to the very end of the book, where you can find special numbers to call some wonderful people, who are all waiting to help.

Introduction

WHY, HELLO THERE.
YOU'RE RATHER WONDERFUL, AREN'T YOU?

(The correct answer to that would be some form of 'Yup, of course I am'. To which I would zap my way over to you if teleportation was real and give you a bone-squishing hug — come ON, World of Physics, what's taking so long?)

I know for a fact you are Rather Wonderful because *you* (yup, *YOU!*) — one of this planet's Most Precious Human People, made up of so many nerve endings, muscles and atomic matter that it boggles my mind — have physically reached up (or down, or over, or across something) to not only wrap your brilliant fingers around this book cover, but actually flick open the pages to read these words.

And not only are you really Rather Wonderful — but I'm also going to make a guess and say that you're A Thinker too. That's someone who uses all the fizzing wires in their brains to notice things going on around them, and to think and ponder and wonder and maybe even worry about why certain things happen — or what could be done to help change the world for the better.

But that's enough guesswork.

I want to find out a little more about you! I mean the *really* important stuff that will let me know if we're set to be book-friends for life. It'll take just two minutes, I promise.
Ready?

If you have one to hand, grab a notebook to write down your answers, or just conjure your responses up in your head, or even whisper them out loud if you fancy it. Whichever way you choose to answer them will be as perfect as can be.

ALL ABOUT YOU

1. Firstly, what is your name? (I know, SUCH an easy question! But it's the starting point for all friendships, so it's incredibly special and important.)

2. How old are you? (If you are a day over 115, I shall be very impressed.)

3. When you were five years old, what was your favourite thing to eat in the whole wide world? (Mine was two crisps with a piece of chocolate in the middle: in other words, a chocolate crisp sandwich! Yum!)

4. Do you have a happy place (real or imaginary, both count!) **— and what makes you feel happiest?**

5. Do you ever get worried or confused or sad sometimes about things happening in our world?

6. If you had to pick THREE things you worry about, or think about, the most, what would they be? (It could be something to do with school, or home, or your town. Or maybe it's a global issue you've heard about on the news. Feel free to tap the side of your head to get those worries out if that helps . . .)

7. Do your worries sometimes feel too big or too difficult to do anything about?

8. Are there any causes you feel passionate about and that make you feel super fired up when you think about them? For example, do you love animals and want to help protect them? Or does the thought of people who are having to live without a house make you want to do something to help? Or maybe you don't like seeing other people being bullied for who they are, and you want to stop it? Why not make a list of all the things you care about and are passionate about — and yes, you can definitely have more than one (I know I do!).

15

9. If you could change one thing about the world, right this second, what would it be?

10. On a scale of 1 to 50,000 (with 1 being the lowest and least annoying and 50,000 being the highest level of annoying it is humanly possible to be), **how annoying are grown-ups?**

11. And finally, do you think I've asked too many questions? (You can write, think or whisper out one of the following three answers.)

yup
nope
IS THIS OVER YET?

PHEW! Well, that got my brain whirring, and I'm sure it's got that incredible head of yours thinking too.

So why am I asking you all these questions?

Well, this is a book about hope, change and making a difference. But if we're going to make the world a better place, first we have to think about the things we don't like about it, the things that we worry about and the things we might feel powerless to change. Because funnily enough, it's those very things which spark the fires in our bellies and makes us want to get up, take action and transform all those frustrations into something good and wonderful.

And by the way, if you've answered a big fat YES to the questions about being worried or sometimes feeling as if everything is too big and difficult to do anything about, then you and I have something in common!

Because I worry a lot too — about the world and all the things happening in it that shouldn't be allowed to happen at all. And I am always wishing I could do more. So you are not alone. Especially as there are *millions* of people of all ages and from all different walks of life who are worrying and wishing too.

BUT I HAVE GOOD NEWS!

Because, as you will see from the following chapters, worrying and wishing is a great and wonderful thing! It's a *gift* — it means you **care**. And every single person who has ever done anything to change our world for the better began exactly where you are now — with worrying and wishing and caring enough to get up and do something about it. And with just a bit of compassion, lots of hope and sprinkles of even the smallest acts of kindness, BIG — nay, GIANT — things can happen to turn those worries and cares into amazing things. I PROMISE. (I only make promises I can keep — especially the ones I make in writing. So this one is a 100% guaranteed, no-returns-ever-needed kind of promise.)

Now I guess it's my turn to share a few things about me and why I'm here typing out these words to you. So here goes . . .

ABOUT ME

1. I'm Onjali (hello again). That's pronounced On-jelly. (And yes, I do love jelly. Strawberry flavoured, if you please.)

2. According to government and hospital records, I'm old enough to be an Actual Real Grown-Up (yuck! Ugh! Gross!). But don't worry. Even though I'm older than you, I'm definitely *not* wiser than you (pssssssst: 99% of grown-ups aren't wise at all. But ssssssssh! They don't want you to know that, so let's keep it a secret).

3. I've been an activist and a feminist from the age of seven. I am now Quite A Bit Older, which means I have been campaigning and marching and fundraising and petitioning for the things I care about for many, many, many years. So I know what it's like to feel frustrated at the Grown-Up World for taking too long and moving too slowly to make the world a better place.

If you're not sure what an **ACTIVIST** or a **FEMINIST** is, don't worry.

An activist is basically someone who deeply cares about making a difference and campaigns to change things — for example, you might be a climate activist and campaign to help prevent **CLIMATE CHANGE** or you might be a chocolate activist and campaign for all children to get chocolate every day of the year. (WARNING: I love chocolate because it is pretty much the best thing on Planet Earth. So this may come up a number of times in this book. Whenever it does, just nod along or, if you agree, give the book or air around you a high-five.)

A feminist is someone who believes men and women should be treated equally in **all** aspects of life. That means believing that all girls should have the same rights and the same access to schools and education and life choices as boys, and believing that women should have equal rights, equal voting and political powers, equal choices, equal pay (did you know that most women around the world are still not paid the same as men for doing the exact same jobs — not even in the UK!) and the same freedoms and opportunities as men. Anyone who believes any of the above is a feminist. I think it's one of the most awesome words to exist and hope you do too!

4. **I get very upset when people are unkind or cruel to others** because they disagree with them or they think those people are 'different' or not as powerful or as important as them. The truth is that every single one of us is different. We are all unique and rather amazing and, thankfully, we aren't exact clones of each other (can you imagine how BORING life would be if that was the case? Yawn). Our differences and uniqueness are what make the world so beautiful. But sadly, **INJUSTICE** (that's when people are treated unfairly) happens when differences aren't respected and people are treated badly or are even made to feel hated for being who they are.

For example, I have beautiful brown skin and can speak and write not just in English but in Bengali too. I also choose to wear lovely coloured scarves on my head to symbolise my religious faith. But sometimes at school, and lots of times even as a grown-up, I have been made fun of or called names or have been picked on because of who I am and what I believe. This is why I feel upset when I see people acting horribly and picking on others too.

5. **I have two organisations that I run with the help of a great many wonderful people.** One helps **REFUGEE** families who have been forced to flee their country and are trying to survive in France and now the UK too. And the other organisation champions the rights of women and girls to live their lives free from all forms of hurt and injustice. But while **WOMEN'S RIGHTS** and **REFUGEE RIGHTS** are two of my biggest passions, I also care deeply about climate change and preserving wildlife and woodlands; about **FOOD BANKS** and breakfast clubs, and all the amazing people helping to keep people who are homeless alive; and, of course, ending all forms of **RACISM**. So as well as my own little charities, I love to support the work of other campaigners and activists too — especially as I believe:

Everything is connected.

Just like all the electric wires that lie behind the walls of a house, and which work together to keep that house running and filled with light, all the world's issues are linked together too. For example, the climate change crisis is directly wired up to the refugee crisis because floods, tsunamis, earthquakes and droughts lead to people needing to flee their homes and lands.

And the refugee crisis has lots of wires linking it up to war, poverty, racism and political bullying, which then each feed into issues such as food poverty, homelessness, and women and children needing extra-special help. Everything is connected, even in ways we can't see. So helping to fix or strengthen any part of the house can help impact all the other parts too.

Lots of people find one single issue or one part of the house they dedicate their lives to fixing. Others find lots of causes and lots of bits of the house they care about. Maybe even at different times of their lives. The magical thing is, there is no 'right' cause or 'one' way to help. They're all important, all linked and all deserving. The decision about what matters most and when, and which part of the house we want to focus on, is up to us. No one can ever decide that for us. So I hope this book will enable you to hone in on your passion — or passions — and help you understand the freedom of choice you have. You can't fix everything alone. None of us can — there are way too many wires to deal with on our own. But if you put your time and energy and love into the one thing or the few things you *reeeeeally* care about, changes can be made, and they will start to fizz and trickle like electricity to help strengthen the house we're all trying to fix.

6. I worry a lot. In fact, some nights I find it difficult to get to sleep because of all the worries buzzing around in my head. But then I remember that no matter what it is I am trying to do or fix, I am never alone. Because the fact is, I get to work with some incredible, wonderful people who give me hope every single day. From those working in food banks and refugee camps to the teachers and volunteers doing everything they can to help the children and people they meet, there is a world of people who have turned their worries into actions and inspired me too. Alone, each of their actions might seem small. But

1+1+1 x infinity

means they are all making endless changes — some without even knowing it. Remembering this fact helps me put my worries — and me — to sleep. And I can't wait to share some stories about these incredible, wonderful people with you so they can help you put your worries to bed too.

7. My happy place is . . . my imaginary chocolate factory!

Preferably one with a huge library where I could sit and read a million books, whilst sipping hot chocolate (of course!). But until I can make this imaginary happy place become a reality, my real-life happy places are: my favourite bookshops, any place I can sit and build something out of LEGO, any seaside in any part of the world and . . . my bed — with an awesome book to hand! Mmmmmmm . . . cosy and delicious!

So that's me in a nutshell. And now that we know each other a little better, I am so excited to get started!

In each of the following chapters, I will introduce you to one of my ten secrets for creating change and making the world a better, kinder place for us all to be in. And the reason I'm sharing these secrets with YOU is because I know you are super-duper-brain-bustlingly clever, and I reckon you are already bubbling with awesome ideas to make things better for people around the globe.

In fact, before we jump into the first chapter, I just want you to know that no matter what you take, or don't take, from this book (don't forget, it's your choice completely), I hope it will help you to remember just One Thing.

(Actually, that's a lie: I'd love for you to remember lots of things. But this is, like, The *Main* Thing . . .)

I hope it will help you understand, without a single atom of doubt, just how magnificent and deeply unique you are. How there is NOBODY on this entire planet like you (not even if you're part of a twin or triplet or even sextuplet and everyone makes you dress the same!). How YOUR voice and YOUR actions can never ever be copied by anyone else because whatever you decide to do is unique to you alone.

And I *really* hope it will help you remember that behind your face and eyes, and within your mind and heart and DNA forged over time and space, you possess a superpower that can elevate your every action and shift worlds you cannot see for the absolute better — should you decide to use it.

That superpower is, of course, kindness.

TWO SYLLABLES.

ONE WORD.

ALWAYS UNDERESTIMATED.

But kindness is always capable of creating huge, earth-shifting changes. And whoah! When that superpower is released into the world along with your unique ways of showing it . . .

SPLASH! BOOM! CRACK! SHUDDER!

The earth's plates (and knives and forks) will shift and alter and move for ever.

I know this because every single day I see people unleashing their own unique powers of kindness to change other people's lives for ever. It's why I know for a fact that there is always hope on the horizon, and that because of hearts exactly like yours, my hopes for a better, kinder world will never fade.

SO LET'S GET GOING THEN. WE HAVEN'T GOT ALL DAY.

Not when your own unique superhuman superpower is waiting to be unleashed . . .

The Five Golden Rules

WAIT!

STOP!

Hold your horses (or cats or dogs or hamsters — whatever is in easiest reach)!

Before you dive hands-first into the very serious business of understanding why something which seems as small as kindness can play such a huge part in your world-changing actions, just a few rules.

Don't worry, they're not rules like 'Sit up straight and don't scratch (or pick!) you nose please'.

They're Golden Rules: which means they're not as boring as ordinary rules that aren't even given a colour (poor things — imagine being so boring nobody could be bothered to assign you a colour).

Think of these rules as the shiny foil wrapper that's wrapped around your favourite chocolate bar. It keeps what is inside fresh and crispy, and you only come across it for an instant before pushing it to the side to get to the actual chocolate (I may be on a secret mission to see how many times I can say the word 'chocolate' in this book. Get counting . . .)

So here are Five Golden Rules I need you to remember as you read:

(Feel free to wear sunglasses for them because, yup, they're just that shiny and important . . .)

1. YOU'RE UNIQUELY YOU, AND I'M UNIQUELY ME

So actions and lessons that may have worked for me might not work for you, or may seem out of your current comfort zone or experience. That's OK. In fact, go ahead and shout 'THAT'S NOT GOING TO WORK FOR ME' at this book whenever you feel like it, and write your own solutions or put in your own experiences instead. Just be sure to let anyone nearby know you may, on occasion, be shouting at a book, and that the book told you to. Just so they don't think you're being strange.

2. THERE IS NO 'ONE WAY'

Well, there are one-way streets that people drive down (those save lives, so please do follow them at all times).

What I mean here is that there is never just one way of taking action or one way of being and doing and believing something. Every single one of the billions of people on this planet are wondrously unique (see Golden Rule 1). Which means every single one of us will have ideas and reactions and visions for helping our world, which may be different. All are equally important and deserving of respect and being listened to. This book is limited because it can only provide you with stories and ideas that are based on my own personal experiences, understanding and skills. And I'm limited because I'm just one person amongst billions. Put simply, my way is just one way of doing things; it's not the *only* way. So please take anything useful from my experiences to forge your own beautiful way ahead, and feel free to tweak things so they work for you. Think of it as me holding out a bunch of colouring pencils I've made for you to use as you want: you get to pick and choose the ones you need and leave the others behind. Easy.

3. STORIES EVERYWHERE . . .

Throughout this book, I'm going to be referring to characters from fictional stories that I absolutely adored at school (and which I still do because they were all *awesome*), who each taught me a great deal.

I wanted to include these stories and introduce you to some of the characters within them because they were my very first launch pads to the thoughts, ideas and questions I had about the world around me. And it's thanks to those thoughts, ideas and questions that I went on my own missions to find answers and people who might help me understand things better.

In fact, without those books and stories, I wouldn't be the person I am, and I would definitely not have become the writer or activist I am. Just like Tintin or Frodo Baggins or Meg Murry or all the children in *The Chronicles of Narnia* books, I wanted to explore the world and find out what I could do to be a part of it and make it better. That's the incredible, eternal power of books and stories — you never quite know where the imaginings and questions they inspire will lead you.

If you haven't read the stories or watched any of the TV programmes I refer to or have no idea who the character(s) I talk about are, first of all, don't worry: I'm not going to be giving any of the story away. And secondly, as far as I can see, you have three options. You can:

(a) *Drop this book like a hot piece of coal* and hit the library/ head to your local bookshop/ask a trusted adult to help find one of my favourite programmes on the TV or online/ask your teacher to see if they have a copy of the book I speak of, so you can devour it right away!

(b) *Shake your head at me, shrug* and just keep on reading anyway.

(c)   *Cheat a little* and ask your parents, carers, teachers or librarians to summarise the books or stories in under thirty seconds (so much fun) . . .

Your choice entirely.

4. GO DEEP-BOOK DIVING, AND COLLECT A STAR OR TWO

Grab that swimming costume, put on your head gear and dive into as much or as little of this book as you want, whenever you feel like it. As this is a non-fiction book, there is absolutely no order you have to follow — so if you want to skip between chapters, you can (yessssss!). Think of it as a strange kind of textbook — only much more fun (as proven by the existence of actual illustrations). Whatever makes you happiest and makes you want to go book diving the longest is great by me. After all, one book dive a day keeps the doctor away (as if *only* apples could do that. Pah! Bet a supermarket manager came up with that lie)!

And regardless of how short or long a time you want to go diving into these pages, remember to look out for some Star Actions on the way. These are actions that you and I can do oh-so easily and every single day to help make ourselves and the people around us — and our planet too — a little happier.

I wish I had real, actual, giant gold star stickers that I could reach out and give you every time you pledged to do one — followed by another, even more giant sticker every time you made your pledge a reality. But then you would probably be *covered* in stickers by the time you got to the last Star Action, and you'd make all the starfish confused. So maybe it's a good thing I can't do that (yet!).

5. THINK OUTSIDE THIS BOOK BOX

At the end of each chapter, I'm going to highlight a real-life person whose courageous acts and great kindnesses impacted history and the world as we know it. Some of them you may have heard of, others you may not have. Either way, I encourage you to not only go and learn all about them, but to explore lots more stories about other people just like them. So ask questions. Hit the library. Become a private detective (PD). In short, please jump beyond what this small rectangular box-shaped book contains and go on your own missions to find lots more amazing stories that lie beyond these pages.

So, now you know the rules, you are free to head to whatever part of the book you like (no more surprise rules from here, I promise). Even if it's just to stare at Isobel Lundie's awesome drawings (drawings are drawn to be stared at, so that's a sub-golden-rule: please do stare at ALL of them for as long as your eyes allow).

READY?
OK THEN . . .
FOLLOW ME . . .

Chapter 1

BE YOUR OWN CHARLIE BUCKET:*
THE POWER OF KINDNESS AND HOPE

*WARNING: This chapter may need to be read
with at least one bar of chocolate to hand.

hope

Deeply wanting something to happen.

I <u>LOVE</u> CHOCOLATE.

HAVE I MENTIONED THIS ALREADY?

AH! But I need to stress just how much I really, really, *reeeeeeeally* love chocolate. (Have you started counting yet?)

I could eat chocolate every day and not get bored. How could I when there are so many varieties to try! So many shades and sizes and shapes! So many different forms of deliciousness available on so many shelves! All shining and sparkling within their crisp, colourful wrappers . . . Yum! (Anyone else hungry already?)

I have loved chocolate ever since I can remember. But for most of my years at primary school, as money was always a little tight in my family, my mum would only let my little brother and me buy a chocolate bar once a week. Which, of course, meant that we would both spend the *whole* week thinking about which bar we would pick and make long, extravagant plans for how we were going to make each of our bars last the longest. It was an adventure to be looked forward to just like any which involves a treat you deeply love.

So when one day, my favourite teacher on the planet, Mrs Koumi, gave me *Charlie and the Chocolate Factory* to take home and read, I felt as if I had found the book of my chocolate-covered dreams. (If you haven't read it yet, may I kindly suggest you follow Golden Rule 3(a) pronto!)

The story, written by Roald Dahl, introduced me to the world of Charlie Bucket: a little boy who loves chocolate almost as much as I do (except he is luckier because he gets to live in a town with an actual chocolate factory right in the centre of it!) and embarks on one of the greatest chocolate-centred adventures ever written. The story revolves around a genius chocolate inventor called Willy Wonka and a search for one of only five Golden Tickets that exist on the *entire planet*! (Even just saying this makes me want to read it all over again!)

Charlie is my first pit stop in this book about hope and kindness, for four reasons:

1. Charlie is one of the very first characters I ever met in book-world who is deeply deserving of the adventure he goes on. Beyond his love of chocolate, at heart Charlie is incredibly and deeply kind to a family that is also incredibly and deeply kind in return. From the way Charlie talks and worries about

his family and grandparents to the way he — a boy with so very little — never complains or tries to make anyone feel bad for not being able to give him what he wants or needs, he is truly the epitome of kindness and **HUMILITY**. (To be humble and possess humility means never ever thinking you are more important than anyone else.) He possess all this, even though he lives a life of incredible hardship and poverty.

2. As well as being kind, Charlie is ever-hopeful. He doesn't give up when he could so easily do just that. In a world where everyone else has so much and he has so little, and where everyone's chance at winning one of those longed-for Golden Tickets is so much higher than his, he doesn't give up hope. He perseveres in saying, 'Maybe I can' in a world telling him, 'It's just not possible'. And anyone who can retain hope in a world of 'no's is definitely a hero in any book!

3. Charlie knows from the start what his passions are: he loves chocolate. And he hates injustice (people not being treated fairly). He knows what he believes in and feels deeply for others too — the true mark of a superstar.

4. I love chocolate (think I may have mentioned it?). Charlie loves chocolate. And I think it's good to be imaginary friends with someone who loves the same thing as you do.

The strengths that Charlie possesses . . .

Hope

Deep kindness

Generosity

Perseverance

Patience

Empathy

Love for his family

. . . are strengths that help him outweigh . . .

CRUELTY   SELFISHNESS

GREED

HOPELESSNESS

INJUSTICE

Charlie's strengths are gifts that I have been lucky enough to see in action, every day, in my various charity works. In fact, I would say there are thousands of real-life versions of Charlie Bucket alive and well and striving for better things all across the planet, even when everyone else is telling them, 'No, it's not possible'. Two such examples are Charlie Whitbread (yup! He is actually called Charlie too!) and Jed Tinsley, who together set up the Mobile Refugee Support team in northern France.

Both Charlie and Jed are heroes who have been working in the refugee camps of northern France for years. They're both rather tall and gangly and love chocolate and books too, and what's more, Charlie has a genius dog called Fozie who loves helping refugees as well! (If Charlie Bucket had a dog, I imagine Fozie would be exactly the kind of dog he would have!)

WHO ARE REFUGEES? AND WHY ARE THERE REFUGEES IN FRANCE?

Refugees are people who have been forced to leave their home, their town or city, and sometimes even their country so that they can survive and be somewhere safe. They are often fleeing war, climate change disasters such as tsunamis, earthquakes and fires, extreme poverty or people from their government trying to hurt them.

Over 80% of refugees stay within the borders of their country or try to find shelter in a neighbouring country. But some try to find family and friends further away or are told to keep moving on until they get to a safer place. Many refugees think countries such as France, Australia, America and the UK might help them, as these countries are signed up to international laws which promise to help refugees. But sadly, those laws are being broken.

For no reason other than racism and fears that refugees might take everything (I know, how silly is that?!), lots of governments don't want to help them at all. Instead, they force refugees to live in forests and parks even in the rain and freezing cold weather, in places where there is no shelter, no water, no hot food and not even any toilets, for months and months and months. They do this in the hope that the refugees will give up and go away. Thankfully, people like Charlie and Jed step in to help refugees and make sure they have everything they need to stay safe and warm for as long as possible.

Did you know: The scientist Albert Einstein, the author Judith Kerr, the singer Freddie Mercury and the Queen's husband, Prince Philip, were all refugees? But thankfully, they were allowed to use their passports and money to get somewhere safe. Not like the millions of refugees today, many of whom have died trying to get to safety because governments refuse to help them.

I met Charlie and Jed in 2016, on my third trip to the refugee camps in France. And the moment I met them, I knew I was in the company of two people who care deeply for others and who are both wonderfully kind. To Charlie and Jed, the refugees they meet are like family, and so, even though they themselves face struggles every day too, they go on giving and sharing what they have with the refugees who need their help most. From tents and sleeping bags to water and socks, from a place to charge their mobile phones each day to a warm coat, they both give and do whatever they can to help the people standing before them. And whilst they're doing this, off Fozie sprints all around the camp, wagging his tail, making children and their parents happy, even if only for a few minutes, by kindly letting them pet him and never ever barking.

To keep on giving what they can, not just for a few days or weeks but for years and years, to a family that may be injured or exhausted or losing hope, makes Charlie and Jed and every volunteer they work with the true Charlie Buckets of this world. Despite some governments and other unkind people telling refugees, 'No, we're not going to help you. Go away!', Charlie and Jed and the Mobile Refugee Support team go on saying, **'Yes, I can help you — come with me and don't lose hope'** to every refugee they meet.

Their unending kindness in the face of so much poverty and need, gifted in a thousand small ways every single day, not only helps to keep people physically alive, but also keeps them feeling hopeful for better, kinder days ahead. The qualities Charlie and Jed possess, that make them both so much like Charlie Bucket, are made up of:

 Knowing what they are truly passionate about (Helping refugees and fighting against the injustice refugees face.)

 Giving what they can with empathy and deep kindness (Some days, they have lots of donations and goods they can give out. On other days, donations are low, so they can only offer advice or lend someone their phone or drive a refugee to hospital. But all of it matters, and all of it is precious.)

* **Never giving up hope** (Charlie and Jed know that although they can't help everyone, even just helping one refugee a day means that there will be at least one more person in the world getting the help and kindness they need.)

The real-life Charlie Buckets of the world are incredible and many. And the great thing is, we all have the potential to be one of them! All we need to do is understand what our passions are, think about how we can use those passions to help others and make sure we spread kindness wherever we are.

CALL
TO
ACTION

HOW TO BE MORE CHARLIE BUCKET

1. Have the courage to learn.

Throughout the story, Charlie is forever asking questions and striving to learn all he can about Willy Wonka and the world of chocolate. By doing so, he gains a rich and deep understanding of both. So be like Charlie and begin researching and reading and asking others all about the issues you are most passionate about. The more you ask and learn, the more likely it is your hopes for making a change will become a reality.

2. Listen to the Grandpa Joes of your world. In the story, Charlie has a friend who shares his passion for chocolate and helps him on his adventures. In his case, it just so happens to be his very funny and incredibly kind Grandpa Joe. We all need a version of Grandpa Joe in our lives — someone who we can share our hopes with and who understands why we want to make them come true. It might be a family member, a friend or a teacher. Wherever you find your own version of a Grandpa Joe — and you may even get lucky and find more than one — listen and learn from them as much as you can. A brilliant activist knows how to listen to others and take on board their experiences, knowledge and ideas, which is just what Charlie does.

3. *** STAR ACTION ***

Be kind every single day. Make it a goal to do at least one nice thing every single day for someone you love and the people around you. It could be . . .

* Telling your parents or grandparents or carers that you love them or giving them an extra thank you for everything they do

* Making something cool for your best friend

* Telling your teacher how awesome they are

* Saving something from your lunch tray or packed lunch to give to someone

* Helping you neighbour out with a chore

* Making sure to leave wherever you've been nicer than when you found it – so that the next person to follow you feels happy (that could be replacing the toilet roll in the bathroom, or tidying up bits of your home or classroom so that no one else has to, or taking care to wipe things up and leave everything as neat as possible in a restaurant)

* Smile – just as often as you like at everyone you meet, and see if they smile back!

TiP: i LOVE MAKiNG LiSTS AND TiCKiNG THiNGS OFF. SO FEEL FREE TO MAKE A KiNDNESS-GOALS LiST FOR EACH WEEK, AND USE AN EXTRA-SPECIAL PEN TO TiCK EACH GOAL OFF ONCE iT'S BEEN COMPLETED!

THE 'BEING MOST CHARLIE BUCKET' AWARD GOES TO . . .

(cue dramatic drum roll please!)

NAME: **GRETA THUNBERG**

ROLE: **GLOBAL CLIMATE CHANGE ACTIVIST AND iCON**

BEING MOST
CHARLIE
BUCKET

STRIKE
FOR
CLIMATE

GOLDEN TICKET QUALITIES:

* **Courage:** Greta began her weekly protests against climate change completely alone and continued despite people making fun of her. She has also voiced her experience with autism, describing it as a superpower!

* **Knowing her passion:** Greta's passion is to stop climate change caused by harmful human actions polluting our planet and to highlight the impact of climate change on the world (including the growing number of climate change refugees).

* **Perseverance:** From being just one girl holding one protest sign, Greta is now joined by the millions of people she has inspired from all over the world, and she continues to hold her protests every single week, rain or shine.

* **Hope:** Greta has never given up her hopes of helping to stop climate change or of developing the skills she needs to speak out about it, despite lots of people telling her it isn't possible or calling her names. Regardless of the many challenges she faces every day to be heard, she continues to voice her wish for governments, businesses and people to work together to save the planet.

Chapter 2

GLADIATORS AND GLADIATRICES . . . AND SHE-RA:

FIGHTING FOR THE THINGS THAT MATTER

warrior

Someone who shows great courage, bravery and strength in their efforts and actions.

HAVE YOU EVER WISHED YOU WERE A GLADIATOR?

You know, like the ones we see in films or learn about at school when we study Roman history? The warriors who were equipped with a sword, a shield and a protective vest, who bravely fought lions and tigers or other people in giant colosseums even though they probably didn't want to do any of those things?

I used to wish I could be as fierce and as brave as a gladiator all the time. Especially when something happened that made me angry or sad, or worried and hurt. Like when I was called names in the playground at school and told 'to go home' because my skin colour and clothes were different to everyone else's. Or when someone made fun of the glasses I had to wear or called me 'Teacher's Pet' just for wanting to get the best grades I possibly could — something the boys at school who also tried hard never got called. Or when my little brother was picked on for the things our wonderful mum used to sometimes make for us in our packed lunches (like yummy okra fingers or a tandoori chicken sandwich or delicious potato bhaji).

Sadly, being bullied, being called names or being tripped up and pushed over was a daily occurrence at school. Even if it was done as a 'joke', it still hurt, and I knew it didn't happen to everyone. So I was very aware from as far back as I can remember that racism and SEXISM existed — even though I didn't really know the name for either of those crimes until many years later.

Racism: Treating a person differently or unfairly because of their skin colour, religious faith or cultural background. This might include bullying and calling someone names or excluding them from things because of how they look, the clothes they wear, the food they eat or the religious holidays they celebrate. From football and sports to offices, playgrounds and our history books, racist actions against non-White people, both past and present, remains a huge and hurtful issue. And it's one which lots of brilliant activists are trying to tackle.

Sexism: Treating a person differently and unfairly because of their sex or gender. This might include stopping girls from going to school, telling them they can't do certain things or not giving them access to the same opportunities as boys — all because they are girls. Later in life it might mean women being paid less than men or, in some countries, not being allowed to vote, marry freely or be in positions of power just because they are women. Sexism can affect anyone, but it usually affects women and girls the most negatively and in the long term too. Linked to sexism, there is also more specifically gender discrimination, which is when someone is treated horribly for how they dress and behave, what they like or don't like, what they think in relation to their bodies, and what society and other people might think is the 'right' or 'wrong' way for someone to act or look. Sexism and gender discrimination are both awful things to experience, and again, there are lots of organisations and activists throughout history and in today's world trying to make sure neither exist.

My friends and I, both at school and beyond it, have all experienced that deeply confusing and infuriating feeling of being treated unfairly or horribly, just for being who we were — whether it was because of our different faiths and beliefs, skin colours, accents, clothes, the food we brought into school in our lunchboxes, and even our sex and the fact that we were girls who wanted to excel in what we did or studied — and even at sports like basketball and football.

These are experiences that, sadly, I know lots of children endure daily. You or someone you know might even be experiencing them right now. If you are, I want you to know that you are not alone, and that you are a s/hero who is perfect just the way you are, no matter what others may say.

No one should ever have to put up with anyone making them feel small or bad or 'wrong' for being different or just for being who

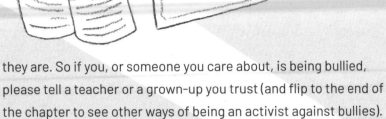

they are. So if you, or someone you care about, is being bullied, please tell a teacher or a grown-up you trust (and flip to the end of the chapter to see other ways of being an activist against bullies). They can and should help you find out where to go and who else to ask to stop the situation from getting any worse.

GETTING HELP

If you want to speak to someone about being bullied or hurt in any way, here are some organisations you can contact.

In the UK there is Childline (0800 1111 or www.childline.org.uk) or Stop Hate UK (0800 138 1625 or www.stophateuk.org). Both organisations are full of awesome, lovely people, many of whom know exactly what it's like to go through what you might be going through.

And if you don't live in the UK, there are plenty of other helplines that are there to help children all around the world.

In India there is the CHILDLINE (call 1098 orchildlineindia.org).

In Australia there is Kids Helpline (1800 55 1800 or kidshelpline.com.au) and Headspace (headspace.org.au).

In New Zealand there is a great organisation called Youthline (0800 376 633 or youthline.co.nz).

But when I was at school, I was unfortunately too shy and embarrassed to tell my teachers or parents about the incidents of bullying taking place, so instead I would imagine myself away. This might be one of the many reasons why I loved reading so much! I loved being able to dive into another world and have my imagination transport me into the lives of other characters whenever I felt like it. From reading old myths and legends like those of the fierce Viking Norse god Thor to diving into comic books about gladiators like Spartacus, I thrived on the hope that one day I too would be just as brave as them and be able to take on anything (minus the swords and magic hammers, of course). There was also one other place I loved to lose myself, and that was in the world of cartoons — and in particular, one cartoon featuring one of the most gladiator-y figures on television! *She-Ra: Princess of Power*. She-Ra isn't technically a gladiator, but she is closer in my mind to what a female gladiator might look like

than any other (at school we never learned about the fact that gladiatrices even existed).

Now, for those of you who are frowning at this book and thinking, 'Huh? How old *is* this author! Who the jumping jackanories is She-Ra?', let me tell you three things about the She-Ra of my childhood — the one who showed up on my very small television set in the 1980s every day at exactly 4.15 p.m.

1. She is awesome.

2. She is like, really, *really* awesome. (I mean, come on! She has a horse that can change into a talking unicorn and a sword that can turn her into a superhuman.)

3. She-Ra's backstory is one of the best stories I ever encountered on TV. The legend behind her existence is that she was born into the royal family of a land called Eternia and is one half of a twin. (Her twin brother is He-Man: Master of the Universe — another superhero who had his own cartoon.) But when she was a baby, she was kidnapped by the evil Hordak and mind-controlled for many, *many* years. When her twin brother, He-Man, finally finds her and helps her discover who she is, she breaks free of Hordak's mind control, transforms into the superhuman version of herself and goes on to fight many an evil force. Now tell me that's not awesome!

I love that She-Ra has two sides to her. The 'normal' side called Adora, and her superhuman side when she uses her Sword of Power to become She-Ra. But as well as being incredibly physically fast and strong (She-Ra could pick up soldiers and huge mountains like they were pebbles!), she also only fights when she has absolutely no other choice, as one of her superpowers is empathy and understanding.

In many ways, She-Ra is just like the legends of Roman gladiators and gladiatrices of the past. Because all of them lived two different lives:

1. As a non-heroic, 'ordinary' person away from the arena

2. As an incredible superhero inside the arena

I have come to meet a whole world of secret gladiators and gladiatrices — and real-life She-Ras during my time as an activist. People who look ordinary on the outside but have a super-heroic side to them that allows them to go and do extraordinary things for others.

And all of them share the same qualities. Qualities that include:

✱ Stepping into the arena — even when they might not really want to . . .

She-Ra and all the gladiators and gladiatrices of ancient Rome might not have wanted to go and fight the forces that were threatening to destroy them. In fact, I'm pretty sure most of them would have loved to have stayed at home with a cup of tea, a good book and a yummy jam sandwich instead! But regardless of how scared they must have been, they still stepped up, took up their swords and tried to fight back. Extraordinary people do this all the time: they try to fight for what is right, even when it might be scary for them.

✱ Fighting back against bigger, unseen forces

In the cartoon, She-Ra has to fight back against actual mind-controlling powers — powers designed to make her stop thinking for herself and prevent her from discovering her true identity. In Roman times, real gladiators and gladiatrices were often slaves or ex-slaves and were treated as outcasts by wider society. Although some chose to become gladiators freely, they were still controlled by their keepers or managers and had to fight for themselves both inside the ring and outside it. So what did they all do? They took one battle at a time.

The real-life She-Ras and warriors of the world also do this every day: they challenge the big, giant, scary issues and injustices of the world — all of which can sometimes feel too big and vast to take on — by tackling one issue or one person or one battle at a time.

✳ Different strengths, one goal

One of my favourite things about all the s/heroes in the books, legends and cartoons I loved best was that none of them ever worked alone. They all had friends — or even family — who they depended on to help them achieve their goals.

In their respective cartoons, both She-Ra and her brother, He-Man, rescue each other endless times in their fight for freedom and their people. Both also have brilliant, loyal friends, and She-Ra even has her amazing sidekick, Swift Wind — her trusty horse who turns into a winged unicorn whenever she is needed. In fact, She-Ra makes friends across all the galaxies and even gets animals to use their specific skills to help her fight evil forces. Similarly, Roman gladiators and gladiatrices often had trainers and mentors, even when enslaved, to help them survive whatever challenge they were about to face.

All of the most super-heroic people I know working in refugee camps or in women's shelters have a world of people around them, who they recognise as fellow superheroes too. They are able to spot and respect the different strengths and gifts of other people and can call on them to come and help them achieve their goals. They all know that *nothing is ever done alone*. Everyone has different skills they can bring to the table. And without those different skills, the battle needing to be won would never even get started. It would be like watching a solo footballer try to score a winning goal against a full team: impossible and exhausting — and likely to be over in two blinks of an eye!

One very real She-Ra/gladiatrix of my world is Lorraine Tabone: a heroine who works incredibly hard every single day to help the homeless people of an entire London district.

I met Lorraine during Christmas of 2019, when a friend told me that a woman living quite close to me needed help gathering food and coats for local homeless people. I wanted to help, so I bought what I could afford and headed down to the address that was given to me, which led to a tiny garage in the middle of endless tower blocks. And there she was, a golden-haired Lorraine, sitting in the middle of endless bags of donations and food,

ordering and shouting and pointing at things and people in all different directions, to make sure everything was getting packed and readied as needed. .

And the very first time I saw her, I knew she was a She-Ra!

No one who meets Lorraine would ever think that she has single-handedly mobilised hundreds of people to help *every single homeless person* across the London Borough of Newham in one way or another — whether that's by providing a bag of food, shoes that don't have holes in them to replace ones that do, a big cosy coat or even a brand-new set of dishes to help a former homeless person celebrate moving into their first and very empty home!

And no one would know that locked away inside Lorraine's mind are the names and histories of every homeless person she has ever met and come to know since she first began helping people in 2015! (That's a LOT of people . . .)

Lorraine doesn't have a sword or a shield, and she definitely doesn't have a unicorn to help her get around. But what she does have is an immense heart, a huge army of volunteers, a magical garage and a trusty old car to help her collect and send out everything a homeless person might need in their most desperate times. Even if that means she has to get up at three in the morning to go and answer a call for help.

HMMMM . . . The more I think about Lorraine and everything she does, the more I think that maybe she DOES have a sword and shield stashed away somewhere safe! I shall have to keep an eye out for them the next time I see her.

You should keep a look out too — because She-Ras, gladiators and gladiatrices who aren't in battle mode could literally look like anyone. They could even look like you . . .

CALL TO ACTION

FIGHTING BACK AGAINST BULLYING

1. **Hone your empathy swords.** If you hear or see someone saying or doing something hurtful or mean to someone — even if it's disguised as a joke — try to imagine what the person being targeted might be feeling and offer them support. Sometimes just knowing that someone else cares is all a person might need to not only feel better, but maybe even gain the strength they need to take action.

2. Make or answer the call for help. No one, not even a real-life gladiator or a cartoon superheroine, could win anything on their own. They need people and experts and friends to help them too. It's incredibly brave to make a call for help when you need it and to recognise that there are some things none of us can do alone. So if you ever need help against a bully or someone doing something wrong, call for it. Ask friends, family, teachers or carers to join forces and aid you. Or if someone comes to you for help, try to help them however best you can — whether that's by listening, helping to find information or encouraging them to call on others too.

3. Use your shield of power. I don't mean an ordinary shield made out of wood or metal like the gladiators used to have. I mean your own personal, awesome shield of power (we all have at least one) that you carry with you all the time, and that you can use whenever you need to protect others and yourself. Sometimes that shield is Hilarious Humour to help lighten a situation and make people laugh instead of hurt each other. Sometimes it's Super-Intelligence and being clever enough to know when you need to ask others for help. Sometimes it comes in Human Form through the shape of friends or family or an awesome teacher who you can instantly call on to help step in and save the day. And sometimes it's Pure Inner Strength and Compassion that make you stand up and speak out against something you know is wrong. Whatever your shield might be, find it, hold on to it and use it when you need to in the best and most beautiful way you know.

4. *** STAR ACTION ***

Inspire your whole school to get talking! Why not ask your teacher(s) at school if they will put on a special assembly about bullying? They could share stories and information about what to do if you or anyone else sees or hears bullying taking place inside or outside of school.

YOUR INNER GLADIATOR/GLADIATRIX

Time to get out a mirror, a notebook and your trusted
pen-swords, and . . .

. . . draw yourself as a gladiator or superhero! And tell us:

Your biggest idea for how to help change this world for the better?

Why your heart feels strongly about your idea?

What strengths you know you possess to make your idea become a reality?

Who you would call on to help protect and defend your idea?

THE 'BEING MOST GLADIATOR/ GLADIATRIX' AWARD GOES TO . . .

(two dramatic drum rolls, please, because I couldn't pick just one awesome warrior for this!)

BEING MOST GLADIATOR/ GLADIATRIX

NAMES: **FREDERICK DOUGLASS AND MALALA YOUSAFZAI**

ROLES: **FREDERICK: ABOLITIONIST MALALA: NOBEL PEACE PRIZE-WINNING ACTIVIST FOR GIRLS' EDUCATION**

GLADIATOR/GLADIATRIX QUALITIES:

✳ **Stepping into the arena:** Frederick began life as a slave in 1818, and after managing to escape his American slave owners, he didn't just go into hiding and try to live a quiet life. He began to use his experiences and his brilliant speaking skills to highlight the injustice and inhumanities of the slave trade. He stepped out into a public arena and spoke in some of the most dangerous places he could, as a Black former slave, to try and stop what had happened to him happening to others.

Malala was like any other ordinary girl who loved her school and teachers. But on 9 October 2012, on her way to school, she was shot and nearly killed by a group of people who do not believe in the equal rights of women and girls. Like Frederick, instead of going into hiding after the shooting, Malala stepped up on to the world stage and has been using her experiences and many skills to stand up for the rights of all girls to have safe access to an education ever since.

Both Fredrick and Malala could have lived quieter, safer lives, especially after the ordeals they survived. But they chose to use their experiences to help others instead.

✳ Fighting back against unseen forces: Racism and sexism are two of the biggest, most serious issues humankind has been battling for centuries past. The crimes committed as a result of people hating someone else because of the colour of their skin or different beliefs, or because of the fact they are girls/women, has led to millions of people being hurt or even losing their lives, both across the centuries and around the world.

But thanks to warriors of the past like Frederick, and warriors of the present like Malala, these issues continue to be heard, learned about and fought against. There are many people who may not know what it's like to live with the impacts of racism and sexism, but by tackling one audience at a time, with one speech at a time, both activists have used their powers of **ORATORY** (speech) to ensure that more people do understand. And that hopefully, once they understand, they will act to stop it.

✱ **Different strengths, one goal:** Frederick and Malala lived in very different times — a whole two centuries apart, in fact! But both share a clear goal in the way they work: to unite people in the fight against the issues closest to their hearts. As individuals, simply by getting up and speaking up about their own experiences and hopes, they have inspired millions — from world leaders to children (aka future world leaders!) — to make a stand on the issues of racism and sexism too. And one by one, like plants springing up in the middle of deserts, their words and calls go on inspiring change.

Chapter 3

SHARPENING YOUR X-RAY VISION:*
SEEING BEYOND THE LABELS

*If you wear glasses like me, be sure to
wipe your lenses for optimum powers!

WHEN YOU HEAR THE WORDS 'X-RAY VISION', WHO IS THE FIRST PERSON TO POP UP IN YOUR MIND?

I can bet you my hidden chocolate coin stash that it's SUPERMAN, right?

(If it isn't, you HAVE to write to me to tell me who else you're thinking of!)

Superman is, of course, a fictional comic-book superhero. He is also a *refugee* superhero, having been sent to Earth as a baby by his parents so that he could survive the explosion that destroyed his planet. Famous for getting his energy from the sun like a man-shaped solar battery, flying through the skies wearing bright blue tights and donning a cape of royal red with his trademark golden yellow 'S' stamped across it, Superman is one of the strongest, fastest superheroes to ever be imagined and brought to life in a story. And he is so famous that I think pretty much everyone on the planet has heard of him, no matter how old they are, where they come from or even if they've never read a single Superman comic book or seen a Superman film in their life!

I can still remember the very first moment Superman flew into my life and imagination. It wasn't through the comic books where his stories first began — as sadly, our schools and local libraries didn't stock them. It was through the classic (very old) Hollywood films starring the actor Christopher Reeve. I was about eight years old and my brother was about six when the moment happened. I remember running to the TV after Mum called me and my brother to the sofa one day in the Easter holidays to watch a film as an extra-special treat. I can remember hearing the theme music **(dun-da-na-na-naaaaaa! Dun-dun-na! Dun-da-na-naaaaa! Dun-da-naaaaaaa!)** blasting out from our very small TV set and thinking it sounded like something exciting was going to happen. And I remember staring open-mouthed, and my brother gasping and giggling in awe, as we watched a man fly through the skies like a missile to help save people.

Safe to say, it wasn't just me and my brother who fell in love with Superman that holiday. Nearly *everyone* at school had watched the film over the holiday too, and what followed was Superman-mania!

From lunch tables to classroom corners, debates raged about Superman's powers and what he could and couldn't do. One boy in my class slipped 'Superman' as an answer into his maths homework (and got detention for it). Another drew an 'S' on to his PE kit. In the playground at breaktimes, my friends and I would wear our coats like capes around our necks and race-fly against

each other, whilst one of my best friends pretended he had heat-ray vision and could melt anything (as long as it was a hot day, we were outside and the thing he had to melt was a bar of chocolate). However, aside from all of Superman's magnificent abilities — his speed, his flight, his strength — there were two things about him that fascinated me the most.

1. The first was his X-ray vision. Before I went to sleep each night, I spent hours imagining I had this skill, and listing the many, *many* things I would use it for (like seeing what was inside everyone's bags at school or finding out all the test answers hidden away in my teacher's desk drawer. How awesome would it be to never fail a test again!).

2. The second was the fact that a simple pair of glasses and a change of clothes is all it takes for Superman — who the *whole* planet knew! — to transform into Clark Kent — the accident-prone newspaper reporter he pretends to be so that no one will ever guess who he really is (I mean, HOW could people not tell???). It puzzled me endlessly that no one guessed right away that Clark Kent and Superman were one and the same person!

These two aspects of Superman's character seemed impossible and too fantastical to ever have anything to do with real human beings. But I have come to realise over time that I was wrong. Because X-ray vision *is* real — and what's more, we ALL have it! We just have to learn how to use it. And it *is* possible for super-kind or super-brave people to be hidden away in plain sight. That's what makes them so special.

LET ME EXPLAIN.

Have you ever met someone who you made guesses or assumptions about, but who turned out to be so much more than you could ever have thought?

It might be someone who is now your friend, but who you didn't really think you would like when you first met.

Or it might be a new teacher in your school who seemed really boring at first, but who turned out to be the coolest teacher ever. It's happened to me lots of times. I think I have someone all figured out, and then they surprise me in the best way possible. Or I find out I was completely wrong about them because I forgot to use my inner X-ray vision to see past my first assumptions. For example, at a charity celebration one day, I met a woman dressed in a dazzling sparkly dress, who was going around the room trying to make everyone dance with her. At first glance, I thought she was one of the leaders of the charity — and someone who loved to dance so much that she didn't mind shouting loudly, even to strangers! But I later learned that she had been homeless for many, many years, and that this celebration was the first proper party she had ever been invited to in her whole life. So no wonder she wanted to dance with everyone and be as happy as she could be!

The best and kindest activists I have ever met have an amazing way of seeing through the façade of things – which means the appearance of things – to understand and see people for who they really are and all the beautiful things they have the potential to be and do. (Those kinds of activists would have been able to see that Clark Kent was Superman in three seconds flat!) That's because they possess a very special type of X-ray vision that can take years to develop and often involves three key strengths. Strengths that Superman/Clark Kent possesses in abundance too, and which revolve around:

1. No judgement

If you ever do read the older Superman comic books or watch the older films, you will notice that even in the midst of catching those who have hurt others and banishing them or arresting them, Superman is interested in hearing their side of the story and their explanations for the actions they have committed. Maybe it's the reporter side of his character who likes to investigate all sides of a story, but in the world of superheroes, he continues to be one of the most curious, non-judgemental and kindest heroes in the fictional universe. Similarly, the greatest activists never judge a person based on a single moment alone, or the way they look or dress or speak. They look behind the label and their actions to learn as much as they can about the person in front of them by letting them tell their story. This is a heroic skill which involves . . .

2. Super-hearing

Of *course* Superman can hear sounds at frequencies that ordinary human beings can't. It's one of the many things that makes him so super, especially as it enables him to hear cries for help that no one else can. Activists who strive to treat everyone they meet fairly not only work hard at listening to people's stories and experiences but can also hear cries for help that might be hidden or buried away in those stories too. That type of super-hearing is incredibly special, and it really does save lives every single day.

3. Hope

Superman's motto was 'Truth, Justice and A Better tomorrow!', which is probably one of the most hopeful mottos anyone could ever live their life by, and which every single activist I have ever met — no matter what it is they are fighting for — lives by too. The hope of a better tomorrow for all the human race.

If I had to do a remake of a Superman film and cast someone I know in the leading role, I know exactly who it would be.

IT WOULD BE NONE OTHER THAN DAN ATKINS: X-RAY VISIONIST SUPERHERO!

Dan is responsible for setting up one of *the* most amazing homeless charities on the planet: a charity called Buses 4 Homeless. It's a charity which turns old double-decker buses into actual, real-life shelters, kitchens and training stations for homeless people. This means that, as well as having a safe place to stay and eat for a few nights, they can actually be helped to find jobs and homes to move on to for the long term.

I first learned all about Dan and his incredible work in a newspaper story (just imagine if it had been written by a real-life version of Clark Kent — who was a reporter for the *Daily Planet!* How cool would that be?).

Dan builds buses and coaches for a living — he is an excellent engineer. But one day after finishing work, he discovered a colleague sleeping inside the luggage storage space of a coach: a sight that broke his heart. Whilst listening to his friend, and hearing how he had become homeless, Dan used his X-ray vision and super-hearing skills to understand that his friend needed long-term help, not just a bed for the night. He was able to look past his friend's homelessness to see that he had great potential and skills that could be used to help him create a better a life.

And as if that wasn't all super-heroic enough, Dan looked at a perfectly ordinary bus — just like the ones we all see in our towns and cities and on telly too — and didn't just see a big old engine carrying lots of seats behind it. His vision transformed it into a place where people could find somewhere safe to stay, make food together and learn. In short, he used his powers of vision to turn something seemingly ordinary and everyday into an extraordinary solution!

So after his friend had finished speaking, Dan marched right out and . . . bought a double decker bus for his friend to stay warm and safe in until he could get the help he needed to move into a home and on to an even better job (which he did!).

Dan often wears a hoodie and a baseball cap as he goes about his daily work — almost as if he is in disguise. And on seeing him, most people would never think that he and his trusted team (led by fellow superheroine Henrietta MacEwan) have been responsible for saving and helping hundreds of homeless people.

But for those of us with excellent X-ray vision, no hoodie could ever mask the cape beneath — or the strengths that make people like Dan the real superheroes of our world.

CHANNEL YOUR X-RAY VISION

CALL TO ACTION

1. Be on the lookout for any opportunity to help someone out — no matter how small the action might seem. It might be holding the door open for someone, or helping pack away the shopping at home, or helping a brother, sister or friend out with their homework. Superman is always on the lookout for ways to help others — even if it's just a cat stuck up a tree!

2. **The next time you meet someone** — especially if it's someone who is new or unfamiliar to you — **try to spot three awesome things about them.** It might be their friendly eyes, the way they laugh and talk, the way they stand or how they look after others. Whether it's someone new to your school, or a homeless person you encounter, hone your vision by seeing past their clothes (or glasses!) and your first impressions of them, so you can be the kind of friend they need.

3. **Be hyper-aware of the labels you give people.** Usually when we meet someone brand new, lots of labels are instantly produced by our brains to help us understand the person in front of us. For example, people might instantly think 'Muslim', 'Asian' and 'woman' when they first meet me, and depending on how they feel about those words, they will react by feeling either happy or worried. It's perfectly natural for our brains to write these labels. But if a label causes a negative reaction that has absolutely nothing to do with the person it is written for, then that can make things incredibly unfair for them. So use your X-ray vision to get rid of labels that scare you, and instead listen to the person first before you write up some new ones.

4. *** STAR ACTION ***

Find your local superheroes. At school or at home, ask everyone in your class or family to help you find out about a local charity which is kind to people in need of help, such as a local homeless charity, a soup kitchen, a refugee welcoming charity or a food bank. And then, when you've found out all about them, think of ways you might be able to help. You could . . .

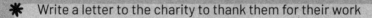

* Hold a special assembly about them in school to raise awareness

* Organise a raffle to help raise money for their cause

* Write a letter to the charity to thank them for their work

* Ask your friends to help you collect lots of presents for the charity at Easter or Eid or Diwali or Hanukkah or Christmas

There are lots of way to help — and I bet you'll come up with lots more! So go for it!

THE AWARD FOR 'BEING MORE THAN ONE LABEL' GOES TO . . .

BEING MORE THAN ONE LABEL

REFUGEE +
SCIENTIST
+ TEACHER
+ HUMANITARIAN
= HIDDEN SUPERHERO

NAME:
ALBERT EINSTEIN

ROLE:
THEORETICAL PHYSICIST, HUMANITARIAN

SUPERMAN QUALITIES:

* **Looking beyond the labels:** Albert Einstein was a refugee who was forced to flee the **NAZIS** during the **SECOND WORLD WAR**, and set up a new life for himself in America. But he wasn't *just* a refugee — like Superman and all human beings, he was never just one thing and wasn't confined to just one label. He was also a great scientist, whose theories and works helped widen human understanding of the universe. He was a teacher, professor and lecturer. And he was a brilliant **HUMANITARIAN** who dedicated his time to helping other refugees.

* **Working for a better tomorrow:** When Albert landed in America as a refugee, he could have easily focused on his own life and not tried to help anyone else. But instead, within a year of arriving in America, he and a group of his fellow refugee friends set up a new refugee-led charity called the International Rescue Committee (the IRC), with the aim of trying to help refugees like themselves find places of safety and get the help they needed. It is still going strong today, long after Albert's death, and is one of the biggest refugee response organisations in the world. It was just one way in which Albert Einstein tried to create a better tomorrow for refugees everywhere.

Chapter 4

BE MORE TINTIN:
LET YOUR QUESTIONS LEAD THE WAY

(Dogs are welcome on your journey — both real and cuddly.)

ask

To say something in order to obtain an answer
or gather information.

OK.

SO I HAVE A CONFESSION TO MAKE . . .

Please don't judge me (see previous chapter), but when I was in secondary school, I was put into detention — TWICE!

(I know, I know. Don't tell my mum. She still doesn't know.)

$E = mc^2$

Both of the detentions were for the exact same thing too: I'd asked a teacher a question that I wanted an answer to.

Now, as much as I would LOVE to say that my question centred on something crucial to all humanity — like how to prevent world hunger or help the environment — I'm afraid my offending questions had to do with . . . maths (ta-da)!

That was because I've always found maths incredibly hard to understand. From something as simple as learning the times tables to figuring out how to divide numbers and carry over remainders or calculate ratios, something in my brain would not allow the numbers to make sense, no matter how hard I tried (and I tried hard enough to somehow get a B in my final school exams.

$\frac{x}{2}$

Which, for me and everyone who knew me, was definitely a miracle!). Give me a dictionary and I will happily memorise words and their meanings in minutes. Or ask me to learn a poem off by heart or read an entire book in one night — easy peasy, lemon and lime squeezy! But maths? Nope! No siree. My mainframe will not compute! It's like asking a chocolate machine to figure out how to make crisps!

This fact was incredibly frustrating for me throughout school — and it was also deeply upsetting for my mum (who is basically a wizard and has three degrees in maths, so couldn't understand why I found it all so hard). I still find it difficult to admit (but you're a friend, so I don't mind telling you) that, even now, maths and I just do not like each other.

So one day in school, when I had just about had all I could take in a very boring lesson about percentages and algebra equations which were just not making sense, I stuck up my hand and asked my teacher why we had to figure out the answers in our heads when the world had already invented a machine to do it for us. That machine being, of course, a calculator!

I guess my question was horribly rude — or at least it seemed like it was from my teacher's point of view. Especially when I stubbornly asked the same question again the next day (oops). But from my point of view, it was a legitimate question. I really wanted to know why things were harder than they needed to be! And both detentions did nothing to get rid of the feeling I had — that there was nothing wrong with my questions at all!

Thankfully, no other question I ever had for my teachers ever got me into trouble. In fact, I would say it was *because* my teachers encouraged me to ask questions that I'm here at all — because my whole life has centred around trying to find answers to things I didn't understand.

Things like why we never learned about women who had helped change the world, or read any books written by them for our exam texts, or why they barely existed in our science books either. I knew there had to be women who had done incredible things — they couldn't all have been sitting around drinking tea all the time! I also wanted to know why people from Bangladesh and other places my family were from (such as Turkey, Yemen and India) were never seen anywhere either — even though I knew, from family stories and books in Bengali at home, that we had **NOBEL PRIZE**-winning artists and thousands upon thousands of soldiers, spies and ambulance drivers who had helped the world win two of its biggest wars. Because sadly, even though millions of men and women from those countries, and so many more from across the world, helped win both the **FIRST WORLD WAR** and Second World War, their roles and names and all the heroic things they did are still missing from history books and films.

As far back as I can remember, I have never been afraid to ask questions. And I think one of the main reasons for that is my love of the Tintin comic books. A love that began in my local library when, aged seven, I saw our librarian (Mrs Martins) putting up a massive new display of all things Tintin one day.

Tintin, just in case you have never heard of him, is a cartoon comic-book character who has a series of adventures in countries across the world. From Egypt to China, from Singapore, Saudi Arabia and Switzerland through to Russia, Tibet and even right up to the moon (!), Tintin travels with his trustworthy and incredibly clever dog, Snowy, on a single quest: to find the truth behind mysteries. And because he is an undercover reporter, finding the truth is always his number one mission.

Tintin has five particular traits that I picked up over time from reading his adventures, all of which made me wish I could be like him. And I often see those five traits mirrored in many of the activists I have come to know and love.

The five traits are:

1. Curiosity: Tintin is *never* afraid to ask the questions he
wants to ask. Whether it is for his job as a journalist or for
himself, he is always curious and interested in finding out
about people or asking what he needs to in order to solve
a mystery.

2. Intellect as a power: Tintin isn't a superhero like the kind
we see in films and other comic books. He doesn't have extra-
-special strength and speed or lots of muscles or magical
swords to transform him into a superhuman. And he never
tries to gain those things or be like anyone else either. He
knows his strength is piecing things together, thinking deeply
and solving crimes. His power lies in his intellect, and with it
he can get himself out of scrapes and bring people to justice.
So that's exactly what he does.

3. Loyalty: One of Tintin's best friends is Captain Haddock,
who often causes more problems than he solves and can be
very rude and grumpy! In fact, Tintin is surrounded by lots of
people who are often quite silly and who I used to wonder why
he was ever friends with. But Tintin treats all of them with

kindness and remains loyal to them — no matter how much trouble they land him in!

4. Compassion: There are many moments when Tintin sees people in trouble and either tries to help them or encourages others to help them. Sometimes he even makes Captain Haddock change his mind about people for the better too. Tintin has a deep compassion for others and wants everyone to be treated kindly — except the criminals, of course! For example, in *The Castafiore Emerald*, Captain Haddock is horrible to a community of travellers who have begun to live nearby. But when Tintin explains what they have been through and how horrible other people have been to them, Captain Haddock instantly changes his mind and offers up his own land to them! Success!

5. Snowy!: Tintin's super-clever dog, who rescues and helps him all the time, is an awesome sidekick to have. And while not all activists have awesome dogs on standby ready to save them from dastardly criminals, most do have someone they can always rely on to help them in their missions.

Reflection

We'll talk more about the incredible importance of friendship in chapter 8, but in the meantime, have a think about who

your personal Snowy is. Who would you trust more than anyone in the world to come on your mission or help you if you got stuck?

It could be a pet or a person. (And yes, mums count too! My mum is definitely one of my most trusted friends in the world and has saved me from lots of mistakes countless times!)
All that matters is that it's a person or creature who you know will be there for you when you need them most.

Now that I think on it, there is another favourite childhood character of mine who shared the exact same traits as Tintin, and who I loved just as much — that was George/Georgina Kirrin from Enid Blyton's *The Famous Five* series. Except George has a dog named Timothy instead of Snowy, and she owns her own island — which I am pretty sure Tintin never did! I spent some of the best hours of maths class daydreaming that I was George, off with my Very Annoying cousins on another great adventure, and thinking of all the great things I would do if someone left me an island of my own too.

Similar to my love of Tintin, one of the main reasons I loved George so much was that she is absolutely fearless and isn't afraid to ask questions either. Her curiosity is what inspires her — much like Tintin — to notice things and ask questions about them. And it's those questions and the quest to find an answer to them that forge the heart of both their adventures.

I have met lots of incredible people who, just like Tintin and George, set off on adventures and quests because of a question they felt they had to find an answer to. One of those people is a phenomenal **NHS** Specialist Podiatrist called Ruhi Loren Akhtar, who asked the very same question I did in 2015, which was, 'what can I do to help refugees?'

What can i do to help?

This one question led to Ruhi asking herself lots more questions. Questions like:

Why are refugees being stopped from leaving war zones and finding safety?

WHY ARE GOVERNMENTS SHUTTING THEIR BORDERS?

Who is helping refugees get hot food and water and everything else they need if governments aren't doing those things?

Wanting to answer those questions for herself, Ruhi began travelling from Newcastle, a city in England, to the refugee camps of Calais in France, and she noticed that refugees were starting to get sick from eating cold, tinned food all the time. So she launched Refugee Biriyani & Bananas! It is an organisation that cooks and distributes thousands of hot meals every week, made up of the dishes and fruits that lots of refugees were missing the most.

A few years later, Ruhi began to hear that refugees in Greece were also needing help and that charities on the ground were struggling to cope. So she left her job in the UK and travelled to Greece to help thousands of refugees a week get the things they need to survive. From wheelchairs and medicine, to tents and sleeping bags, to her gift of home-cooked meals. These are all adventures that her seemingly simple questions have led her on. And all adventures I have come to learn of, love and support through my own questions, which, over time, led to me meeting her too.

So never be afraid of your question, because who knows what incredible adventures and amazing people their answers might lead you to.

CALL TO ACTION

GETTING YOUR QUESTIONS OUT INTO THE WORLD, TINTIN-STYLE

1. If you could ask someone super important three questions, what would those three questions be?

2. If you could send your three questions to someone who you think should be able to answer them, who would you send them to and why?

3. *** STAR ACTION***
Write a letter to a person of power.

If you answered question 2 with 'the Prime Minister', 'the Queen', 'my MP (Member of Parliament)' or even 'the President of [name your country of choice]', you can ask an adult to help you find their address, and actually post your questions to them!

So if you did pick one (or all!) of those people, why don't you do just that? Write your questions out using the template on the next page, save up or ask for a stamp and send your letter out into the big wide world! You never know where your words and questions might land or what adventures and new questions they might lead you to!

[Your address — so they know where to send a reply to]

[Date]

Dear [insert the name of your Very Important Person],

My name is [insert your awesome name — not Tintin's!],
and I would like to ask you three very important questions. These
are questions that matter a lot to me and, I think, must matter a
lot to you too. They are:

1.

2.

3.

I look forward to hearing from you soon and reading your reply.
Thank you.
Yours sincerely,

[Your awesome name again]

THE 'TINTIN QUESTIONING AND INTELLECT' AWARD GOES TO . . .

TINTIN QUESTIONING AND INTELLECT

NAME: **OPRAH WINFREY**

ROLE: **AMERICAN TALK SHOW HOST, TELEVISION PRODUCER, ACTRESS, AUTHOR AND PHILANTHROPIST**

(someone who likes to support good causes)

TINTIN QUALITIES:

✷ **Curiosity:** If anyone in the world knows how to ask questions fearlessly, it has to be Oprah Winfrey, one of the world's most famous talk show hosts. From US presidents to international music, film and sports superstars, and from authors to members of the British royal family, there is no one famous that the Queen of the Talk Show hasn't asked questions to in interviews — except for, perhaps, the actual Queen herself (maybe one day!).

* **Intellect as power:** Oprah is also viewed by many as one of the savviest women on the planet! As the first Black female American billionaire, she has used her intellect, her knowledge and her skills to make financial investments and grow new ideas, projects and ways of making money. And not only has she done all this, but she also uses her money to help others, setting up schools for girls in parts of Africa and gifting millions to different charities around the world.

* **Compassion:** If you have ever been afraid to show how you feel in public, then Oprah will certainly make you feel less afraid! As well as her intellect and curiosity, Oprah is famous for being honest enough to show her emotions on screen, especially when she is interviewing someone who has moved her and made her cry from joy or sadness. She is unafraid of her feelings or of showing her compassion — a fearless skill which makes those she interviews feel as if they are being deeply and truly listened to.

* **Snowy:** Well, I don't think Oprah has ever had a dog called Snowy (yet!). But she has lots of dogs, who I am sure would all rescue her if she ever got into a scrape or two.

Chapter 5

STRENGTHEN YOUR LIGHT:
NEVER BE AFRAID TO ASK FOR HELP WHEN YOU NEED IT

unite

To join with others or bring people together for a common purpose or action.

When I was in primary school, there was one game I loved playing above all others during breaktime, and that was football-rounders.

As you may have guessed from its Incredibly Clever name (or having played it yourself — so much fun, right?), the game was simply Ordinary Rounders, complete with four bases and played by two teams, only instead of a tennis ball, we used a football. And instead of having to hit a smaller ball with a bat or a hand, you had to kick the football away just as far as you could before you made a run for it. It was so much more fun than Ordinary Rounders — and great for anyone (like me) who had to wear glasses — after all, a big football coming your way is much easier to spot than a tiny little fuzzy ball.

My friends and I couldn't get enough of football-rounders, and whenever someone brought their football in for the day, we couldn't wait for lessons to finish so we could head out and start up a game. But one day, in the midst of a week of glorious football-rounders games every breaktime, something happened that stopped everything in its tracks: a group of bullies from upper school began to pick on us whenever we started a game. One afternoon, they snatched our football and ran off with it. Meaning that . . . THE FOOTBALL HAD BEEN KIDNAPPED.

REPEAT.

THE FOOTBALL HAD BEEN KIDNAPPED!

Now, just to give you some insight into how devastating this was for us, footballs were precious things and, when I was at school, far rarer and more expensive than they are nowadays. Especially if they were a special blue one like the one that was kidnapped had been. So whenever anyone had a football at home that they were actually allowed by their parents to bring into school for us all to play with, everyone — and I mean *everyone!* — looked after it and respected the owner as if he or she was a king or queen, and the football their crown.

So when the football was snatched from us, we were shocked! And we all knew that poor Benjamin, the owner of the football, was going to get into a whole world of trouble with his parents. There was no way he could just go out and buy another one because he didn't have enough pocket money saved up — or a job (apparently school is more important!). And not just that, but as I mentioned earlier, his football was blue. *Blue!* AND it was a birthday present from his grandad. Which meant it might as well have been a diamond because that's how special a football it was to him.

Benjamin knew he was in a world of scrapes. He HAD to get that football back. And before home time too!

Reflection

If something that was yours was taken by someone unfairly, what actions would YOU take to get it back? Who would you ask for help and how would you persuade them to help you?

In hindsight (which means looking back at something a long time after it has happened), Benjamin could have gone and told a teacher. But the on-duty teachers were busy helping someone who had fallen over and scraped their knees badly, and I think in his mind Benjamin felt as if he just didn't have the time to wait! So instead, Benjamin put out a call for help and began to ask not just us — his immediate friends — but anyone else in the playground who might be able to help, to join him in getting his football back.

What happened next was so awesome that it still makes me smile!

Nearly everyone Benjamin asked for help said yes! Mainly because Andreas, the head bully, had kidnapped lots of people's things and never returned them — even when ransoms had been paid! So within a few minutes, nearly half the playground had joined Benjamin's army. Some of them genuinely wanted to help, others were curious to see if a fight was going to break out — and not wanting to miss it if it did!

Following just a few steps behind Benjamin, we gathered forces and all watched as he shuffled up to Andreas, who was busy bouncing the kidnapped ball against a wall. Benjamin must have been terrified, but he managed to ask for his ball back loudly enough for everyone to hear.

To this day, I can still hear the silence that fell all around us, as we each held our breath and waited to see what Andreas and his friends would do.

After a few seconds of looking confused, Andreas began to laugh and then told Benjamin to get lost.

And that could very well have been the end of this Kidnapping Incident.

But then Melanie, and then Raj, and then me, and Bobby, and Sharon, and most of those who had promised to help began to shout out, 'Give him the ball back!', 'It's his ball!', 'We want the ball back!' at the top of our voices. Something we would never have done if we had been alone.

We must have looked and sounded like a group of squawking seagulls, but it worked! We were so loud that everyone else in the playground began to notice us — including the on-duty teachers. And before they could reach us, Andreas shouted back, 'Fine! Here! Take your stupid ball and get lost!', before kicking the ball to the other side of the playground.

VICTORY!

WE HAD A VICTORY!

It was short, sweet and wonderful, and within a few minutes we were right back to playing football-rounders as if nothing had ever happened.

The whole event took place within one short breaktime. And looking back, I can't help but think how clever Benjamin was to ask others for help. He could very easily have tried to take on Andreas on his own, but there was no way that would have worked — and chances are, either he or his football — or even both — might have been hurt.

But by putting out the call for help and not being afraid to signal to his friends that he needed us, he united us against a common enemy, trusted us to keep our promise and got back what was his safely and swiftly — and without his parents or grandad ever finding out that he'd briefly lost his ball!

Benjamin's brave action reminds me of so many of my favourite stories, in which someone is helped to overcome an enemy because they are courageous and clever enough to recognise they need help. In fact, I don't think there's a single story that I loved in which the main character doesn't undertake that very action! From the wonderful Bobbie, a girl in E. Nesbit's The *Railway Children* who isn't afraid to call on a whole village to help her, to Arthur Conan Doyle's genius detective, Sherlock Holmes, who relies on everyone from the homeless communities of London to his good friend Watson to help catch criminals, the very best s/heroes are forever calling on the skills and gifts of others to see a story through to its end.

But one of the best, most exciting literary examples of the power of asking for help that I encountered on my school library shelf has to be the epic, dimension-splitting adventure undertaken by Meg Murry in *A Wrinkle in Time* by Madeleine L'Engle. I can still remember reading the story underneath my bed-covers — conveniently shaped like a tent — and breathlessly turning the pages to see if Meg could do it: if she could call on all the forces she needed to save her father and the world from IT and the Black Thing — powerful shadows seeking to rule whole worlds (if you haven't read or heard of this story, I would urge you to run on over to your school library and ask your librarian all about it, pronto!). On her adventure, Meg learns that:

1. There is nothing wrong with asking for help. Not just for others, but for yourself too.

2. Every single person you meet has the potential to teach you something (especially schoolmates, and even annoying little siblings).

3. Going on a time-travelling adventure is way more fun when you're on that adventure with others instead of being alone.

4. Five heads, or more, are better than one (especially if three of those heads belong to a Mrs Whatsit, a Mrs Who and a Mrs Which)!

5. The Black Thing, the IT, the darkness — whatever you might call hurts, pains, worries and anxieties that threaten to rob you of your energy, spark and light — can all be banished with the help of not only those who know and love you, but kind hearts waiting to advise you. All you have to do is reach out.

I'm not sure if Benjamin ever read *A Wrinkle in Time*, but if he did, I imagine he would have seen quite a lot of himself in Meg and her endless capacity to seek and accept the help and wisdom of others.

Either way, I think I learned a lot from Benjamin, because my women's rights and refugee aid work always involves doing exactly what he did in the playground at school that day: putting out calls for help in the hope that people will join us and help us. Whether it's finding information that I need to help get a mum and her children to a **refuge** (a safe place to stay) or asking for people to come and help deliver aid in refugee camps, I can only be useful when other people — all very different and often far more skilled than me — answer my calls. Anything I do is deeply

reliant on others helping
me. And through asking
for help, I have had the
honour of meeting and
learning from some true
leaders — people who have
never been afraid to signal
to others that change is
needed, and who have
worked to unite people to
fight for a cause.

One of those people is the
brilliant Marissa Begonia
— a woman who has been
fighting to help thousands
of overseas domestic
workers (people — mainly
women — who are brought
into the UK by richer
families to work for them
as nannies or cleaners
inside their homes) from
being abused or hurt or
forced into slavery by their
employers.

HUMAN SLAVERY IN TODAY'S WORLD

Human slavery is sadly not something that just happened a long time ago. It continues to exist even in today's world and is, in fact, the second largest illegal 'trade' on the planet. It involves men, women and children of all ages and backgrounds being trapped in all kinds of unpaid and abusive roles. It often involves overseas domestic workers — people brought from overseas for jobs in a country far away from their own — being mistreated and hurt and unable to get back home. Sometimes overseas workers are trafficked (transported and bought and sold illegally) and used as slave labour on fruit or vegetable farms, in clothes factories or as servants in rich homes. Often, they are promised wages that are never paid and have their passports and documents and even phones taken away from them so that they cannot run away or ask for help. Some are physically harmed and locked away until the person who 'owns' them no longer wants them. There are at least 40 MILLION people across the globe estimated to be working as slaves (lots of organisations think the real figure is much higher). From chocolate plantations in Ghana to the mineral fields of Columbia whose goods make up our mobile phones, from rich households in London to farms and factories across every country, slave labour continues to be used — and fought against.

Using her own past experiences as an overseas domestic worker, Marissa has bravely spoken out against the many types of abuse and hurt she experienced. Born and raised in the beautiful Philippines, Marissa had hoped to find a job so that she could look after her three children, send them to a good school and give them everything they needed to have a happy life. But sadly, in the Philippines, there were no jobs that paid enough for her to do this, so she left her children behind to become a domestic worker, first in Singapore, then in Hong Kong and then in London. She took the jobs, even though she would have to be away from her family for long periods of time, in the hope that she would work for nice families and could send the money she earned back to her children. But instead, some of her employers began to hurt her or stopped paying her, knowing that she couldn't afford to go home and that she had no one else to help her. Luckily, she eventually managed to escape and found a family who treated her well.

After her escape, Marissa realised that there were lots more women like her who were being hurt and made into slaves by the families they were working for. So she set up a brilliant organisation called The Voice of Domestic Workers. This charity calls for justice and basic human rights for all of the UK's 16,000 overseas domestic workers. Being the only organisation of its kind in the UK, it provides a safe place for survivors of abusive employers to talk about their experiences and seek help. It delivers English, art and educational classes, and helps survivors find other jobs or take on legal cases against the people who have hurt them. Marissa even takes women who have escaped particularly horrible families, and who have nowhere else to go, into her own home to care for them. There are amazing people just like Marissa working in many different countries around the world to help save women and children who are domestic workers from being hurt by their employers. From India's National Domestic Workers' Movement to Australia's Walk Free campaign to the International Domestic Workers Federation working across Europe and other parts of the globe, there are thousands of people trying to make sure that s/heroes like Marissa are not tackling this huge issue alone.

I met Marissa many years ago, at a talk being given about women's rights, and within a few minutes of meeting her, she asked me to join and support her campaign — just like Benjamin did in the playground all those years ago. Ever since then, I have had the honour of marching with her outside the UK Parliament and the UK Home Office, and have also seen her speak in front of politicians in an effort to help make the government give domestic workers the same worker rights as everyone else (such as the right to a fair wage, payment for work, access to medical help or the right to change employers). I have even danced with her at an event called One Billion Rising — a global day where women across the world unite to demand an end to violence against women.

Marissa's actions over the years have helped unite thousands of people who want overseas domestic workers to have their human rights recognised, and she has personally helped save hundreds of lives too. And it is thanks to her endless courage to go on asking people to help her in her work that she has the capacity to do all of this.

I think activists such as Marissa are like human lighthouses. They put a spotlight on something wrong which needs to be made right, and they send out a ray of light into the night every time they ask for help. Over time, gradually, one by one, other lighthouses switch on to answer the call, until suddenly they number thousands and flood the darkness that used to exist. The fact that I get to help Marissa spread that light, and see all the many lighthouses working hard to shine for her cause, makes me hopeful that one day the justice and human rights she is striving for *will* be heard and made into a reality.

GATHERING YOUR FORCES OF LIGHT

1. Identify your cause. If you had to choose just one issue you wanted to do something about right this minute, what would that issue be? It could be something like ending the use of plastics to stop climate change, or wanting to help refugees in some way, or wanting others know about the different kinds of human slavery still going on in the world.

2. Imagine you're dialling an emergency number and have just thirty seconds to ask someone for help in relation to your chosen cause: what would you say and what would you ask them to do?

3. *** STAR ACTION***

Create your call! Some of the greatest activists are also some of the greatest speech-writers, artists, poets and singers of the world. From the US president Abraham Lincoln, who acted to end the global slave trade and inspired people through countless speeches, to the Grammy Award-winning Malian singer Oumou Sangaré, who uses traditional music to sing about women's rights, there are endless ways to unify people for a single cause. Pick one way in which you would like to shine a light on the issue you care about, and go create it! It might be a:

poster

song

poem

painting

speech

story

bake sale or your very own fundraising drive

Or something else entirely . . . Whatever it is, create and share it with your family or friends, or at school, and see what happens . . .

NAME:
NELSON ROLIHLAHLA MANDELA

ROLE: ANTI-RACIST REVOLUTIONARY, NOBEL PEACE PRIZE WINNER AND FIRST BLACK PRESIDENT OF SOUTH AFRICA

LIGHTHOUSE QUALITIES:

✳ In 1948 the government of South Africa introduced a racist set of laws called **APARTHEID**, which forced Black people and White people to lead separate lives. Under these laws, Black people were not allowed to live in the same areas, share a table in a restaurant, attend the same schools or even sit on a train or bus with White people. Even before these laws were created, Black people were not allowed to vote in elections, and many were forced to live in poverty. Nelson Mandela did not agree with any of these things, and he joined a political party called the African National Congress (ANC) to help defeat and change these unfair rules and laws. While he was a member of the ANC, Nelson became famous for his speeches and his ability to unite millions of people behind the cause of racial equality. And he continued his work in secret even after the ANC was banned.

✳ Nelson was arrested for his efforts and imprisoned for 27 years in total. But even while in prison, he never gave up hope, and he became a symbol of anti-apartheid and unity against racism around the world. Sparking global protests at his being jailed, Nelson was released in 1990 and spent three years working to legally end the horrible apartheid system. The last apartheid law was finally abolished in 1993, and in that same year, Nelson was awarded the Nobel Peace Prize. Then, in the first ever election where Black people were allowed to vote, he became the first Black president of South Africa!

* His light continues to shine on long after his death through the Nelson Mandela Foundation, which helps people understand and work for equality and peace — together. One of his most famous sayings was:

As we let our own light shine, we unconsciously give other people permission to do the same.

Chapter 6

FACING THE TWISTS AND TURNS OF YOUR YELLOW BRICK ROAD:*
DON'T EVER GIVE UP HOPE

*Feel free to wear/hold anything covered in glitter for the duration of this chapter.

perseverance

To continue in the efforts to do or achieve something,
even when this is difficult or takes a long time.

I would absolutely love to tell you that being an activist is easy. And that trying to make a change in the world for the better, or trying to help someone, can be achieved without difficulties getting in your way (I mean, who would ever want to stop you or anyone else from trying to do such wonderful things?).

But I don't want to lie to you. And I also don't want you to put this book down thinking that any person who is famous for their great achievements or skills — whether they're a world leader, a singer, an actor, a sports star, a scientist, an artist, a human rights activist or an author — hasn't failed at least once in their lives or been blocked by all kinds of seemingly impossible obstacles. Obstacles I often liken to the challenges Dorothy faces in *The Wonderful Wizard of Oz* — the famous story in which a little girl called Dorothy and her dog, Toto (another heroic dog sidekick!), are whisked away by a tornado to a magical land called Oz.

There they are told they must defeat the
Wicked Witch of the West in order to get
back home — a seemingly impossible
task for someone who has just landed in
a place she never even knew existed! On
her journey to do just that, Dorothy meets the
Cowardly Lion, who is seeking courage, the Tin Woodman, who
is seeking a heart, and the Scarecrow, who would love to have
a brain. Not to mention lots of flying monkeys and the Wicked
Witch herself, who attempts to literally throw Dorothy off course
as she tries to reach her goal!

Anyone who has ever tried to create, bring or do something new
in the world are like real-life versions of Dorothy. All of them are
travelling down a special road that leads to a dream they want to
see become real, and all of them are knocked off course at some
point.

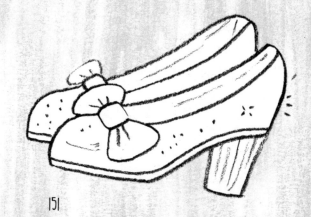

Look at international superstar Beyoncé, who could easily have given up when her original girl band, Girls Tyme, lost in a huge American TV talent show called *Star Search*. But even after losing on television in front of millions of people, Beyoncé didn't give up. She set up a new group called Destiny's Child instead, which continued even after two of her friends decided to leave.

Now she is a record-breaking Grammy Award winner many times over and continues to be one of the biggest pop stars on the planet.

And what about Bill Gates, who invented Microsoft after all his other products failed . . .

And Elvis Presley, who was told he couldn't sing and took up a job as a truck driver until someone realised that he could . . .

And Oprah Winfrey, who was fired off a TV news show . . .

And The Beatles, who were told they would never succeed because no one would ever listen to guitar music again . . .

And Vincent Van Gogh, whose artwork now sells for millions, but who produced over two thousand paintings whilst struggling with poverty and mental health issues . . .

And the suffragettes of Britain, including Emmeline Pankhurst and Sophia Duleep Singh, who fought for women's right to vote, despite being jailed and punished and threatened, and who eventually went on to win!

I could go on and on and on. In fact, if I had to make a list of everyone famous who had failed before succeeding, I would probably break the world record for creating the longest list in history.

Reflection

Speaking of lists, why don't you start one of your own? Make a list of three famous people — they can be from any time in history or be living right now — who you are a fan of. And then go and find out what happened to them before they became famous, and what failures, hardships or rejections they had to overcome to become the person they wanted to be.

SO WHY AM I MENTIONING FAILURE IN A BOOK ABOUT HOPE?

SIMPLE.

Because having hope is easy when things are going well and the yellow brick road ahead looks sparkly and clear. But it's when things are *not* going well that we need hope the most — when we have moments of feeling like huge failures, and there are tornadoes and flying monkeys and all kinds of strange and unexpected things trying to stop us from reaching our goal.

If I had a penny for every single time I have had that sinking feeling of having failed, I'd have enough to buy my own plane! I had the feeling in school, when I came last in a two-mile country relay race and nearly made my whole team lose.

I had it in college on exam results day, when I failed to make the grades I needed to get into my chosen university (a place I had dreamed of going ever since I was seven). Having never ever failed on such a huge scale before, I was absolutely devastated and felt so embarrassed and ashamed that I think I cried for a whole week!

And I had it countless times when trying to be an author. In fact, right this very minute, in my room, hidden away in a bright red suitcase, are all the rejection letters I received from agents telling me my stories weren't quite good enough for them to want to work with me.

And as for my charity and activist work . . . Well, there isn't a week that goes by without a new problem to tackle, or something else I wish I could do, or a fundraising target I haven't met.

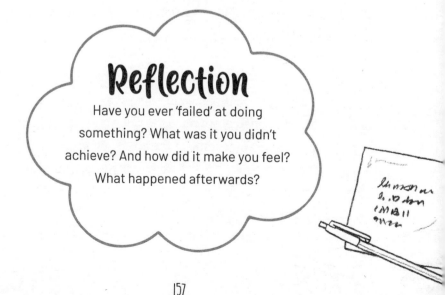

Reflection

Have you ever 'failed' at doing something? What was it you didn't achieve? And how did it make you feel? What happened afterwards?

But (and here's where the sparkly glitter comes in!)

for every failure I have had, and continue to have, something new and wonderful happens.

In fact, I would say that without all the things that went wrong in my life, I wouldn't be the person I am or have so many things I never expected to happen go right!

So yes, I came last in the school relay race. But my being last meant my relay race partners had to run faster and harder to catch up with the other runners (we ended up coming third!). And one of them ran so fast and so hard that she got noticed by a local sports trainer and asked to join a regional runners league! (You're welcome, Jody!)

And nope, I didn't get the grades I needed to go to Oxford University (a place I had dreamed of going ever since I was seven). Instead, I ended up going to the University of Wales in Aberystwyth, where I met some of the best friends I will ever have and a teacher who inspired me to explore feminism more and hold on to my dream of going to Oxford (I ended up getting in on my third try and went on to study women's rights because of her). And every rejection letter I received from agents telling me they weren't interested in my stories made me go back and try to make my stories better. And because I kept on doing that, I ended up meeting the best agent anyone could ever have and now I get to write books like this one! How incredible is that?

And as for my charity and activist work: I have come to accept there will be good days and bad days. But with the bad days, instead of being scared or upset, I now feel excited. Because I know they're going to lead me to thinking up new solutions that I would never have thought of otherwise and meeting new, incredible people who will help me reach the place I need to go. In short, every failure has been a test to see if I have the heart, courage and brains to keep going. Just as all the failures you might face will be too. All you have to do is remember that, just like Dorothy, you have the power to call on those you meet to help you on your way.

Oh — and that you're wearing some pretty awesome glittery shoes made just for you, and which only you can ever walk in. (They might be invisible to others, but that doesn't stop them from existing!)

CLICKING YOUR HEELS AND TURNING FAILURES INTO SUCCESS

1. Think of the very last thing you think you 'failed' at. It might have been getting something wrong in class or not getting good grades or coming last in something. What did you do afterwards or what are you doing to make sure the same result never happens again?

2. List all the unique skills you have that might help you solve an unexpected problem.

3. In *The Wonderful Wizard of Oz*, Dorothy helps the Cowardly Lion find his courage, the Tin Woodman find a heart and Scarecrow to stop being scared all the time. What one strength would you want her to help you find? And how could you go about making that strength become a reality for yourself?

4. Click your heels for real and whisper the following words three times:

There's no such thing as failure, only lessons in how to do better

Because sometimes it's just fun to remind ourselves of what we can use our heels for.

5. *** STAR ACTION***

Find your courage and share your failures with others. At school or at home, ask your teacher or parents/carers to do a 'Failure Five' with you once a week. That's where you all sit down together and take five minutes to write a list of the things you feel you might have failed at. Then, share them.

(WARNING: Grown-up failure lists will be waaaaaay longer than yours! So be sure to factor in more time for them.)

Sharing what you think of as failures with others will not only make you feel better, but it will make everyone around you feel better — and make those failures seem teensy-weensy too. A great activist is not afraid of sharing their failures, because they know it might help others have the courage to move past whatever obstacles they might be facing and not feel so alone. And I think you might even be surprised at how other people view what you think of as failing too, or the things you can learn from each one. So go for it! And laugh, giggle and even cheer your Failure Fives, so they can be acknowledged, learned from and then moved on from swiftly.

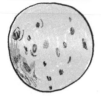

DOROTHY
BOUNCING–
BACK—FROM—
OBSTACLES

THE 'DOROTHY
BOUNCING-BACK-FROM-OBSTACLES'
AWARD GOES TO . . .

NAME:
MARY JACKSON

ROLE:
**AEROSPACE ENGINEER AND
MATHEMATICIAN AT NASA**

$E = mc^2$

$\dfrac{x}{2}$

THE HEART, BRAIN AND COURAGE CODE:

✳ Born in 1921 in America at a time when the **SEGREGATION** (the separation and unequal treatment) of Black people was widespread, Mary was determined to use her skills at maths to become something that few non-White people — let alone women — were allowed to be: an engineer. Her brilliance led her to work in the segregated women's computing team (run by Dorothy Vaughan — the first non-White woman to be promoted within NASA to lead a team), where she went on to become the first Black female engineer. Despite experiencing constant racist and sexist abuse, Mary reached the highest levels of engineering it was possible for her to reach and continued to work for NASA for 34 years.

✳ During her years of work, Mary noticed the constant **DISCRIMINATION** and mistreatment of women and decided to do something about it. So after 34 years of working in the highest engineering position available, she abandoned it and took a demotion (a lower role with less pay) to become the manager of a new Federal Women's Program. There, she worked tirelessly to ensure women mathematicians, engineers and scientists of all colours were hired and promoted across many organisations. Her actions and sacrifices contributed to the global women's rights movement and helped a new generation of women enter jobs and roles that they had not been allowed to access before.

Brains, great heart and courage made Mary a revolutionary and helped not just her hopes, but many women's hopes and dreams finally come true.

Chapter 7

THE CHRONICLES OF . . . YOU: FLEXING YOUR EMPATHY MUSCLES AND BEING A RIPPLE-STARTER

ripple

The continuing and spreading results of an event or action.

A week after my seventh birthday, something Pretty Wonderful happened.

On our weekly trip to the local library (my mum took me and my brother every single Friday or Saturday so that we could choose books and max out our library cards), another librarian we loved, Mrs Burnham, had something waiting for me.

'I heard it was your birthday last week . . . So I got this for you,' she said, holding something out to me. 'It's for you and your brother to read together — and to keep. Happy birthday . . .'

Mrs Burnham always reserved books or comics she thought me and my brother might like, and she was always giving my mum lots of tips about which murder mysteries were the best ones to read (I think my mum secretly wanted to be a detective!). But she had never given us a book to actually keep before!

The book she was holding out to me, with a tiny silver bow stuck to its cover, was called *The Lion, the Witch and the Wardrobe*. It was written by an author I had never heard of: C.S. Lewis. And on its cover it had an image of a queen with a huge crown and a pale white face; a loud, roaring lion; and a lamp post with a little girl standing beneath it.

TO SAY I COULDN'T WAIT TO READ IT WOULD BE AN UNDERSTATEMENT.

I HAD to read it right away! So, with a very shy 'Thank You!', I ran over to my favourite chair and began devouring it. The epic adventure of the Pevensie children — Lucy, Edmund, Susan and Peter — who find a whole other world through the doors of a wardrobe, with creatures and talking animals aplenty, had me hooked from the very first page. And as soon as we got home, I carried on reading.

Teatime came and went, and I couldn't stop reading. Night fell and my favourite programme on the TV came and went, but I still couldn't stop reading. Even after Mum had sent me and my brother to bed and switched off our bedroom lights, I didn't want to stop reading — so I didn't. Instead, long after Mum thought I was asleep, I climbed up on to my window ledge and kept reading by the light of the lamp post on the street outside (a lamp post that my imagination told me looked exactly like the one Lucy Pevensie finds on the other side of that wardrobe! For those of you who have read or seen the story, you'll know what I mean. For those of you who haven't, I would suggest you drop this book IMMEDIATELY and go borrow/buy/watch/ask about this story right away. No matter your age, you will not regret it).

The Lion, the Witch and the Wardrobe quickly became — and remains — one of my most favourite books. I desperately wished I could be Lucy, the youngest of the Pevensie children, and the one who, despite often being bullied, forgotten and thought of as the weak child by her brothers and sister, is responsible for not only discovering the world of Narnia (the mythical land on the other side of a wardrobe!), but, through her instinctive empathy, kindness and bravery, setting off an incredible, life-changing series of events!

Reflection

FLEX YOUR EMPATHY MUSCLE

Empathy: When you do your very best to understand and share the feelings of someone who has experienced something you never have, or who is living a life completely different to yours. It's a very special skill, and one of the greatest superpowers any of us can have.

NOTE: **Empathy is *not* the same as pity or compassion, which is simply to feel sorry or sad for someone. It goes one step further. It calls on you to use the deepest pockets of your imagination so that you can visualise and feel what it might be like to be that person.**

For example, it could help you understand how cold a homeless person might be feeling on a wet and stormy night. Or how hungry someone who hasn't eaten all day might be feeling and what they would love to have. Or how frightened a refugee child new to your area or school might be.

Some very famous people such as the Dalai Lama (the spiritual leader of Tibet and of lots of people around the world), the incredible poet Maya Angelou, the legendary author Harper Lee (who wrote one of the greatest books of all time, *To Kill a Mockingbird*), Mahatma Gandhi (famous for using non-violent methods to free India from British rule) and even singing superstar Dolly Parton, all understood that empathy is like a muscle — one that needs to be strengthened and used in order to understand others. It's the power that is needed *before* you act in a deeply kind or brave way, because only those people who have Real Empathy will sacrifice their energy, time and money to help someone they don't know. It's a power every single activist, like you, has. And it's up to you to decide when and how to use it.

I don't think you would be here, reading this book, if your empathy muscle wasn't already super strong. But if you want to keep flexing it, here's some questions you can ask yourself . . .

1. When was the last time you imagined what someone or something else might be going through and feeling — and why did you want to do that?

2. Have you ever read a book, or watched a programme or film, or listened to a song that has made you cry? Or perhaps made you feel a bit funny from sadness or happiness (or both)? If so, what was the name of the book, programme, film or song, and why do you think it made an impact on you?

3. Who is the person you most admire in the world for their empathy muscle? (It could be a celebrity campaigning for something or a teacher at school or someone at home.) Why do you admire them so much — what do they do to show other people that they care about them?

Lucy discovers the world of Narnia all by herself. But as anyone with brothers and sisters will know, it's almost impossible to keep a secret from them! And it's sometimes even more impossible to have them believe a word you say — especially if you're the youngest!

In the story, Lucy tries desperately to make her siblings, Peter, Edmund and Susan, believe that there really is a magical world lying right inside the wardrobe of the house they have been sent to. And that the creatures of that world need their help. But when she isn't believed, she goes back to see how she can help on her own. Sadly, she is betrayed by someone she loves in lots of awful ways: a betrayal which leads to one huge, dreadful event that had me sobbing over many a page.

But like all people with deep levels of empathy, Lucy doesn't hate the person who has hurt her. She tries her best to understand and forgive in a way that the kindest of people often do: with their whole heart.

Throughout the story, each of Lucy's actions, her quiet, deep faith in herself — even when no one else seems to have any in her — and her forgiving, kind heart make her the true heroine of the story. Despite being the smallest of her siblings, she is the reason

why an entire world is discovered, epic battles are fought and a wise, talking lion is met. In short, Lucy is what I call a Ripple-Starter: the seemingly small and ordinary character who causes endless, magical ripples to change things in ways that even she can't see or predict.

Every single story has a Ripple-Starter at its heart. And I don't just mean in books and in films, but in real-life too. Because here's the newsflash:

You are the Ripple-Starter in your world and your story!

And I am the Ripple-Starter in mine. And every person ever born is a Ripple-Starter in theirs, setting off actions and feelings and consequences in a million and one ways that they can't and might never even see.

The real trick is to make the ripples we create the very best of the best that we can possibly release. The kind of ripples that will reach out and make people we may never meet feel incredible and hopeful, even when they might be going through a tough time, and even though they might never know who is responsible for a particular ripple effect reaching them.

For example, Mrs Burnham, my lovely librarian, could never have guessed how much her incredible gift of a book would mean to me. She probably couldn't have imagined that not only would I read her gift over and over and over again (and still do), but that it would lead me to secretly test out the back of wardrobes in my aunts' and uncles' houses endlessly, in the hopes that I could find Narnia too. Or that I would borrow all the other *Chronicles of Narnia* books from the library and love them so much that they made me want to make up my own stories in the hopes that one day, I might be a writer. That was just one of Mrs Burnham's ripple effects on my life — and who knows just how many she released?

I am very lucky to see and work with and meet Ripple-Starters every day of my life. People who are often the Lucys of their worlds —

sometimes ignored and belittled, even bullied for trying to make others see what they see — but who go on with their deeply empathetic actions regardless. Some very young Ripple-Starters even made it into my second book, *The Star Outside My Window* — a story about an incredibly brave girl called Aniyah and her little brother Noah, who find themselves suddenly without their mother and living in a foster home. Much like Lucy, Aniyah's self-belief, and her courage to find what she believes is her mother's star, changes not just her world and Noah's, but that of everyone around her.

All the children in *The Star Outside My Window* have to survive in a world without their mums and dads. Not through any fault of their own, but because of something that is happening at home from which they need to stay safe — a something that involves someone else intentionally hurting them or making them feel scared and unsafe.

There is a name for that something, because sadly, it happens in a lot of places around the world. That name is 'domestic abuse', and as with all things that hurt people, it is illegal and wrong and unacceptable.

WHAT IS DOMESTIC ABUSE?

Domestic abuse is when someone bullies, tries to control or acts violently towards another person or people that they know — often their own family members. But just as no one is allowed to be a bully at school, no one is allowed to be a bully at home either. Which is why there are lots of people trying to stop domestic abusers, and even more trying to help survivors of abuse get away from the person hurting them and find somewhere safe to stay. Domestic abuse can happen to anyone, but overwhelmingly happens to women and children. It is a crime, and no one should ever have to live with it.

If you, or anyone you know, is being bullied or hurt by someone in their homes, there are lots of people waiting to help. You can call Childline on 0800 1111 or confidentially message for help or advice at www.childline.org.uk.

In my story, Aniyah and Noah, and their new foster brothers and sister, Ben, Travis and Sophie, have all seen different ways in which domestic abuse can happen and have been brought to live in a foster home so that they can stay safe and be loved by a foster mother. All of them were inspired by the many children I have met in women's shelters and refuges — children who are incredibly brave and who are having to find friends and homes in places that are strange to them. And although none of them really know it, all of them are Ripple-Starters — children who are changing things and even helping to catch bullies with their courage and self-belief.

Luckily, there are lots of people trying to help children like Aniyah, Noah, Ben, Travis and Sophie. All of them are incredibly brave and deeply kind, and they remind me of Lucy from *The Lion, the Witch and the Wardrobe* all the time. Not just because they spark endless change that will help others in ways that even they don't know, but because they push open doors and walk through them, no matter how frightening or hard it might be.

One of the real-life Lucys I have had the honour of getting to see in action is a woman called Karen Ingala Smith. She has bright, frizzy brown hair, wears vibrant red lipstick and glasses, and is one of the quietest, kindest and most deeply empathetic people I have ever had the honour of meeting.

She runs a charity which helps women find safety and shelter after they have been hurt and can't stay in their own homes any more. But not only does she help lots of women by giving them a roof and a bed and all the things they might need to feel like

themselves again, she has also had a very specific ripple effect on the world that I find incredible.

BECAUSE, YOU SEE, KAREN IS A REAL—LIFE DETECTIVE!

Not the kind of detective that runs around in a long coat with a magnifying glass in her pocket and a fake moustache on her face (although that would be quite funny to see!).

She is a patterns-detective. That means she gathers lots of information and evidence and finds patterns and signs that she can use to help protect — and even save — people from the actions of very dangerous bullies.

You may have seen films or read stories about cool detectives and police officers who try to find criminals and sometimes even murderers so that they can be caught and put in jail. And even though Karen isn't a police officer and she doesn't call herself a detective at all, she does something incredibly unique to help them all do their jobs better.

You see, a long time ago, Karen began to notice that lots of women who had tragically been hurt and bullied so much that they had been killed, were never talked about on the news or the radio. Their names and stories were missing, and no one knew anything about them. She was shocked by this and didn't feel that it was right. Especially not for the family and friends and children of these women, who were now having to cope with losing someone they loved being taken from them.

So she began to collect reports and ask questions so that she could tell the world the names, ages and stories of all the women who should have been helped and saved, and have them be known and remembered and counted by everyone. And the more she counted and shared and remembered, the more Karen began to spot patterns . . . Patterns in the way the criminals — the abusers — had acted.

Karen believed that the behavioural patterns she had spotted would help the police catch these criminals sooner, but no one would listen to her. In spite of this, she continued doing her research. Eventually, and with the help of a few kind — and very clever — friends, Karen was able to produce a document that proved her findings, with facts and figures that no one could ignore.

Karen could very easily have given up every time she was ignored or told to go away during the many years of her work. But she continued working hard and trying to share her findings because she knew her actions might help others. Thanks to Karen's tireless efforts, she has begun a **REVOLUTION** (a huge and complete change) to the way police, news reporters and even government ministers understand and identify domestic abuse patterns.

I met Karen a year or two after she had started her work, and when I was struggling and feeling alone. The strength of her kindness and her deep empathy for what I was going through — even though she had never experienced it herself — helped me launch Making Herstory, an organisation which helps women and children running away from people trying to hurt them to find safe spaces to stay and get help and justice too.

Whenever I feel tired, or so exhausted that not even my favourite bar of chocolate can give me the energy I need, all I have to do is think of Karen, and I immediately feel better. It's one of the many ripple effects she continues to have on me and the hundreds of women and men and children she has helped across the country too.

In *The Chronicles of Narnia*, Lucy is given a cordial that can heal wounds, and which helps her save people. It's a fitting gift for a Ripple-Starter like Lucy, whose empathy and kindness make her constantly want to help and save others. It is, after all, what the very best ripples can do: they can save people, even with just half a drop of kindness and care.

Any activist and Ripple-Starter I have ever met, whether in real life or in the pages of a great story, always reminds me of two things:

1. That there is no such thing as an action too small — because who knows where that action might lead and how it might make others feel. Whether it's a smile given to someone having a really bad day, a listening ear for a friend who's upset, passing on a book you love to someone who might love it too, or gifting pennies, lunch food or goods to someone in need of them, the ripple effects of our actions can never be underestimated.

2. That every single one of us is connected to each other through what we do and how we make others feel. Karen's ripples impacted me directly in lots of ways, which in turn will have impacted others around me, like my friends and family.

And they may have gone on to share or pass on that impact to others around them — and so on, and so on. It's as if every single one of us is a domino, standing in a world of never-ending, criss-crossing dominoes whose force fields can make us switch directions or impact us in ways we can't see, and who we can impact and change too, in ways we can't fully imagine.

So take notice of your incredible actions — every single one of them has an impact, even if you can't quite see it. Make it your intention every day to send out only the very best ripples you can muster, so that your very own chronicles (your own records and story) and adventures are as exciting and as magical as any story you will ever be gifted.

CALL TO ACTION

MAPPING THE CHRONICLES OF YOU

Have you ever heard of a spider map?

It's a map that joins lots of things together in one single picture.

For example, bus maps and underground train maps, which are often colour coded and seem to have lots of arms and legs, are all spider maps. They're my favourite kind of map! So I'm going to ask you to create one, just for you!

To get started, you'll need a sheet of paper and lots of colouring pens! Once you have those, here is what I want you to do . . .

1. In the very centre of the page, draw . . . YOU. However you want to look. You can be wearing a crown. Driving a cool car. Waving a wand. Whatever you like!

2. Above your drawing of you, write out three things you would like to do this week that might make someone else happy. It could be making your mum or dad or carer a cup of tea. Or helping a brother or sister out with their homework. Or doing your own homework on time! Or smiling at ten people in your class. Anything you like!

3. Now, from each of those three actions, I want you to use all your different coloured pens to draw links to all the things that *might* happen as a result of what you plan to do and all the people who *might* be impacted by your one action. For example, if you make someone you love a cup of tea, it might have a direct impact by making them feel surprised and happier than usual. Which might mean that they go to work or go about their daily chores feeling much more joyful. In which case, they may go on to be nicer to the people they meet that day — who themselves might go on to make others feel happy too!

4. When you have reached the end of your map and there's no one else you can possibly think of who might be touched by each of your actions, count the number of possible impacts that each of your three actions might have. (Be sure to count yourself and how it makes you feel too!)

5. *** STAR ACTION***

Start your own ripple. Choose one action that is the easiest and simplest to do from the three you have highlighted on your map and . . . go out and do it! And see if any of the ripple effects you thought might happen actually do! You might even hear or learn of other people your action touches — so be sure to add them to your map as you go!

THE 'BEING-MOST-LIKE-LUCY-PEVENSIE' AWARD GOES TO . . .

BEING-MOST-LIKE-LUCY-PEVENSIE

NAME: MARCUS RASHFORD

ROLE: FOOTBALLER AND CHILD FOOD POVERTY ACTIVIST

JOINING UP WORLDS TO HELP OTHERS:

Up until March 2020, Marcus Rashford was just another Manchester United and England footballer. But as the global pandemic led to businesses and schools shutting down, he began to realise that lots of children in the UK who were suffering from **CHILD FOOD POVERTY** — which is not having enough food to eat at home — would be left with no help. Especially as **FREE SCHOOL MEALS** (a programme through which children are given free lunches at school) was something that the UK government was trying to get rid of too.

Using his own childhood experiences of food poverty, Marcus launched a campaign to help ensure free school meals would still be provided to children, even during school holidays and throughout the pandemic. He wanted to make the government change its mind about ending the free school meals programme too. He joined a charity called FareShare to help raise money, and within three months he helped raise over £20 million to help supply millions of free meals to children across the country!

But that's not all. What started off as a simple campaign to keep free school meals going led to businesses, cafés, restaurants and supermarkets joining the campaign too, and giving away millions of pounds worth of fresh food to children and families in need. And this is something that lots of businesses are still continuing to do.

The huge success of this one campaign led Marcus to begin working on other issues that children and families need help with too, such as access to books and stories, for which Marcus has launched his very own book club. And tackling racism in literature and football, so that all children can see themselves as belonging to both fields.

Very much like Lucy Pevensie, Marcus's empathy for the children he wants to help, his kindness and his self—belief has led to the joining-up of whole worlds to ensure that those who need help get it and are known about. In his case, this united businesses and charities and even government ministers who had never worked together before!

The ripple effects of all his work will be felt for many, many years to come by all the children and families Marcus still goes on helping — a fact that was recognised by the Queen herself, who, in 2021, gifted him a medal for all the endlessly wonderful ripple effects he has had on the world.

Chapter 8

FINDING YOUR OWN SAMWISE GAMGEES:
THE IMPORTANCE OF FRIENDSHIP

For my birthday in 2021, one of my Very Best Friends in the Whole Wide World gave me what I think might just be the Best Birthday Card on the Planet.

On the cover of the card is a drawing of Frodo Baggins and Samwise Gamgee, and floating above their heads in capital letters, are the words:

I LOVE YOU MORE THAN SAM LOVES FRODO!

Now, just in case you have absolutely no idea who Frodo Baggins or Samwise/Sam Gamgee are, let me enlighten you and bring your attention to one of the Most Fantastical Trilogies to ever have been written by a human being. (For those of you who do know: well done. You and I are definitely Book Buddies!)

Frodo and Sam are characters from an epic fantasy world created by the writer J.R.R. Tolkien, and they take centre stage in a trilogy called *The Lord of the Rings*. Whilst the trilogy was written for older readers, it follows on from a children's book Tolkien wrote called *The Hobbit*, in which he introduces readers to the world of . . . well, hobbits: an imaginary race of people who are half the size of human beings, have super hairy, thick feet and love to eat as many times in a day as they can (which makes them sound just like all the uncles in my family!).

Whilst *The Hobbit* and *The Lord of the Rings* are completely different stories, they are cleverly linked together by first the finding of a powerful golden ring (in *The Hobbit*), and then the huge burden of destroying it (in *The Lord of the Rings*)! This task falls on the little shoulders of Frodo Baggins: a brave hobbit who, even though he doesn't really want to, accepts the life-changing task of trying to rid the world of the terrifying ring. And that's it! That is ALL I am going to tell you. To say anything more would mean I would have to stand trial for ruining one of the best stories created for you and your future self.

But whilst I won't tell you any more of the story, what I will do is highlight the incredible friendship between Frodo and his gardener, Samwise Gamgee — a friendship that faces many a test, and without which the story would not exist as it is.

I didn't read *The Lord of the Rings* until I was in my late teens, but when I did, I recognised instantly just how heavily Frodo's future is entwined with that of the one friend who follows him, for better or for worse, on the journey they have to take. It forges the heart of the trilogy, and around it are lots of other friendships on which the entire mission rests too. Friendships between different people belonging to different races (such as the dwarves and elves), which are pushed to the absolute limit of endurance.

Friendships are, of course, the basis of most of the best stories we will ever read. Think of your favourite stories or films, and I'll bet all the pages in this book that there is someone who helps the main character in some way — whether they're real or make-believe, whether they're a stranger who pops up for only a few seconds, or whether they are another major character like Grandpa Joe in *Charlie and the Chocolate Factory*. (And don't forget animals . . . flying unicorns and little dogs also appear a LOT as amazing sidekicks and friends.)

Reflection

FRIENDS-ALERT!

Let's test my theory out, shall we? Think of your most favourite ever character in your most favourite ever story (it can be in a book or film or TV show), and answer the following questions:

1. Make a list of all the people that help your favourite character on their journey (you can use your fingers to count them if you like).

2. What characteristics do the people who help your favourite main character share? For example, are they:

brave?

good listeners?

kind?

HUMBLE (NEVER THINK THEY'RE MORE IMPORTANT THAN ANYONE ELSE)?

able to come up with clever solutions and ideas?

determined?

HELPFUL, EVEN IF IT MEANS THEY MIGHT GET IN TROUBLE?

funny?

loyal?

NOT AFRAID TO SAY SORRY IF THEY DO SOMETHING WRONG?

always hopeful?

THE KIND OF PERSON WHO WOULD GIVE YOUR FAVOURITE CHARACTER THEIR LAST EVER CHOCOLATE BAR (OR AT LEAST SHARE IT!)?

3. And finally, how do these other characters change the course of the story — what might have happened (or not happened) without them?

See! Every character ever written has friends or people who help them on their way. And even though we might call them or think of them as 'side' characters or less important characters than the person or creature actually on the adventure, their existence is incredibly important.

I think one of the reasons we love our favourite stories as much as we do is not just because of the main s/hero, but because of all the other characters and friends they meet along the way too. Sometimes those friendships are made between animals (like the pig Wilbur and the spider Charlotte in E.B. White's genius story *Charlotte's Web* or Pumbaa and Timon, who befriend Simba in Disney's *The Lion King*). Other times they are characters of completely different ages and who you would never think could ever be friends (like the old, grumpy Tom Oakley and the frightened Willie in Michelle Magorian's beautiful book *Goodnight*

Mister Tom). Occasionally, friendships might even spring up between living and non-living figures (like the friendship between a character called Owen and a statue in the park in Lisa Thompson's *Owen and the Soldier*).

And I have no doubt that one of the reasons I loved *The Lord of the Rings* so much was because of Sam's unfailing love and support of Frodo — qualities which make him a hero of the story too.

Pretty much every superhero/ine and s/hero, both fictional and real, is only able to do what they do thanks to the friends they have. People they can trust, and who they can call on to help them too. Even if it's only for a moment and in the short term.

Because the truth is, trying to help others or save worlds can be incredibly hard work. And no matter how big or small or seemingly easy your goal, you are likely to face lots of hurdles and obstacles and worries as you go. Whether it's trying to get enough people to sign a petition you launch, getting a letter written and sent to your MP, raising money and goods for a particular charity or simply deciding on what might be the best course of action to take — all of it requires you to look to other people for help or guidance and knowledge.

There is not a single amazing activist I have met who has ever achieved their goals solo. From helping to distribute posters to having volunteers jump on board and stay for months or even years on end on a particular cause, to be an activist you need to find potential Samwise Gamgees to help you with your quest — no matter how long or short that quest might be.

And here's the awesome fact that I want you to know: there are Samwise Gamgees waiting to help your inner Frodo absolutely everywhere. They might not have hairy feet (which is no bad thing), but versions of Samwise are definitely out there — and you may even have some by your side already.

Some of them might pop up and help you for a short time like a mysterious creature of kindness, never to be seen again! Others might stick with you through thick and thin and for years on end, and be with you no matter what happens (often known as a Best Friend For Ever . . . And Mum!).

Some may disagree with you or have a different idea about what to do and how to do it — and that's OK. Because you can both learn from each other as you go off to do your own things (after all, there is never just one way to do something or make a change). And some might join you for part of your journey before they have to go their own way, which is perfectly fine too.

The trick is learning to spot a True Samwise Gamgee and enjoying their company for just as long as you have them by your side. They're quite easy to spot. Here are some tell-tale signs:

1. They always make you feel good about yourself and help to take your worries away by listening to you.

2. They have the same passions as you do — so you both have lots to talk about all the time!

3. They make you laugh or think about things or see things differently. And they definitely do all three if they're a Super-Sam!

4. They always want to help you. Even if others might think your ideas are a little crazy!

5. You can trust them, one hundred, thousand percent, to tell you the truth.

6. They don't leave you when things get hard.

7. When something wonderful happens, they are one of the first people you want to share it with!

Your gut will always tell you when you've met A True Samwise Gamgee in your life. It's a deep feeling, way, way down in your belly, that makes you feel happy and excited and comfortable whenever you're with them.

Just in the same way that your gut will tell you when you've met what the world calls a 'fair-weather friend'. This is someone who sticks around for the good things but jumps ship and runs away when things get too hard. Often, when you've met one of these types of friends, your gut and tummy might feel a bit funny, and you might feel uncomfortable and suspicious and not want to be with them for too long. So trust your instincts as you go on your journey. Because as you pursue your passions and try to make a difference to the causes that matter most to you — whether it be food poverty or climate change or something totally different — the journey you go on will lead you to meet lots of new people. People who will hopefully become friends, and who will encourage you to keep going, even when things seem hard and your energy might be waning.

When you care about an issue deeply, it's normal to sometimes feel tired, scared or anxious that you won't be able to help or make a difference. And it's normal to sometimes feel like you want to give up. Whenever those moments happen, I want you to remember that you are not alone and that some of the greatest people on the planet have those moments of doubt too.

Whether it's Abraham Lincoln, the US president who had to witness his country going to war as he tried to legally end human slavery; or Sophia Duleep Singh, a British Indian suffragette who saw women around her being hurt and arrested for wanting the equal right to vote; or even David Attenborough, who, at the age of ninety-seven, is still trying to make politicians listen to him about climate change, all of these people, at some moment in their lives, will have wondered whether it was worthwhile to keep going and will have questioned themselves over whether or not they had the energy to go on. (Luckily for all of us, they did and do!)

And if Frodo had a pound for every time he wished he was back home and not having to make a journey he didn't want to be on — well, he'd be quite a rich little hobbit.

And if I had a pound for every time a friend has rescued me, then I'd have enough to buy my very own hobbit-hole to live in!

Because it's at those exact moments of nearly giving up or losing hope that true friends come to the rescue!

From being short on fundraising targets and asking friends to spread the word and donate, to asking for their advice on a difficult campaign, or simply joining a friend for tea and cake and a good laugh (or cry, depending on how everything is going), I feel incredibly lucky to be surrounded by lots of amazing friends who step in to be there for me when I need them. And all of them started off as strangers who shared my passions and likes, and who, over time, came to be some of the most important, wonderful friends I could ever ask for.

One of these special people is a woman I met in 2015, after she contacted me by email to ask if she could come with me to the refugee camps of Calais in France.

I had absolutely no idea who this woman was, and she had no idea who I was. But she had heard online that I was about to leave for my first ever trip to France, and she trusted me enough to want to join me.

Her name is Yasmin Ishaq: a mother of six children, who lived all the way in the north of England (hours and hours away from me),

and who, like me, had never been to help in a refugee
camp either.

I don't know what it was — maybe it was the lovely words in her
email and her honesty about the fact that she had never worked
in a refugee camp either — but Yasmin's email instantly made me
feel as if she was someone I could trust to join me and my other
friends on our first ever aid convoy (a group of people taking
emergency goods and food to people in need). So I wrote back
and, not knowing what on earth to expect, told her that she was
welcome to join us.

Ever since that first trip, Yasmin has been with me on nearly
every single one of my refugee aid convoys to France. She was
there on that first day when we landed and I didn't really know
where to go or how to fully help people. She was there for some
of the most important meetings which led to the launch of
Maison Sesame (a project that takes in and looks after the most
vulnerable refugees from the surrounding camps, and gifts
them a shared house to live in until they can move on). She has
fundraised and goods-raised tirelessly since 2015, and one day
she even rang to tell me she had bought a van — a huge white van!
— that she was going to practise driving so that we could take
out more tents and sleeping bags and piles and piles of coats and
shoes and food!

In short, the person who messaged me out of the blue to say she wanted to help me in my work all those years ago has proven herself to be one of the truest, most loyal friends anyone could ever hope for. And if it weren't for her brilliant abilities to listen and advise me on my next crazy idea, and to laugh with me when things go wrong (because they often do!), and her endless trust in me, I'm not quite sure O's Refugee Aid Team — our organisation — would even exist, let alone do everything that it now does.

Of course, it doesn't hurt that she is also a huge fan of *The Lord of the Rings* and one of the few people in my world who completely understands why I have a Frodo cloak hanging in my closet.

So keep your eyes and ears and heart open for the Samwise Gamgees of your world.

Who knows where they'll come from or how long they can stick with you on your quests.

And more importantly, remember to be one right back, won't you? Because being the best kind of friend you can be to someone who is one to you, will make each and every journey you go on so much more fun and awesome than it otherwise would be.

CALL TO ACTION

BEING A SAMWISE GAMGEE

1. Let's use our imaginations to the max for this one! Imagine that you are a hobbit — hairy feet and all! And are about to set off on one of the most dangerous missions of your life — complete with strange creatures and angry beasts who are after you. You have just one person from your world that you can take with you. Who would they be, and why? What have they done to prove that they might be the right person for you to take with you?

2. Now let's reverse it. Imagine someone you love, or who you think of as a best friend, has to leave their home — possibly for ever! — to embark on a life-threatening quest. You want to go with them, but have to highlight why you — out of all their friends — should be the one they take. What kinds of things would you say about yourself to make sure they picked you?

3. When was the last time you helped someone? Who was it? And why did you decide to help them?

4. ✱✱✱ STAR ACTION ✱✱✱

Escalate your friend radar. Is there anyone you know who needs help — or a friend — right now? If so, think of three things you might be able to do to help or be a friend to them, pick one, and then go for it!

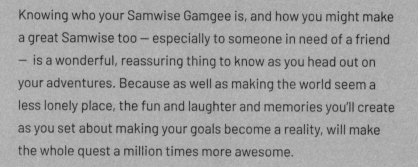

Knowing who your Samwise Gamgee is, and how you might make a great Samwise too — especially to someone in need of a friend — is a wonderful, reassuring thing to know as you head out on your adventures. Because as well as making the world seem a less lonely place, the fun and laughter and memories you'll create as you set about making your goals become a reality, will make the whole quest a million times more awesome.

THE 'FRODO AND SAM' AWARD GOES TO . . .

NAME:
AYAAN MOOSA AND
MIKAEEL ISHAAQ

ROLE: GOLDEN BLUE PETER
BADGE-WINNING REFUGEE AID
FUNDRAISERS

TWO BEST FRIENDS, ONE WORLD—CHANGING JOURNEY:

Some people are incredibly lucky — they meet their Samwise Gamgees early on in life and know right away the exact type of adventure they both want to go on!

Such is the case with Ayaan and Mikaeel, two best friends who, in 2020, aged just seven years old, decided to set up a simple lemonade stall on their street to raise funds for child refugees in a country called Yemen. Refugees that they had learned about through the news, and who they wanted to help.

Asking their parents, aunts and uncles to help them, they both began to sell their homemade lemonade to local people — calling their stall 'Lemonade for Yemen Aid'. Within a few months, they became so famous for their efforts that they began to be sent letters and donations from people all around the world — including a letter and donation from the Oscar Award-winning actress and UNHCR ambassador Angelina Jolie! (UNHCR stands for United Nations High Commissioner for Refugees, and it is a globally funded agency which raises awareness of, and supplies basic survival kits to, refugees across the world.)

In under a year, Ayaan and Mikaeel raised over £100,000 for the children of Yemen, and they are continuing on their epic quest to help people displaced by conflicts in Gaza in the Middle East too. Their efforts led to them being awarded a rare golden Blue Peter badge and inspiring lots of children to set up their own 'LemonAid' stalls too.

In fact, one day soon we may even see a global LemonAid Day, where LemonAid stalls raising money for refugees pop up on streets across the world.

And all because two best friends came together and used their friendship to help make a change for the better, from something as simple as a bag of lemons . . .

Chapter 9

PROTECTING YOUR FORCE FIELDS:
HOW TO DEFLECT NEGATIVE FORCES

force field

An area of energy that surrounds an object or place.

Did you ever wish you had a super-heroic
power to hand that you could do incredible things with?

Maybe you've dreamed of using the Norse god
Thor's hammer to harness the power of lightening?

Or maybe you've wished you could make extra-strong silken
strands zoom out of your wrist like Spider-Man so you could go
swinging through your town like a . . . well, spider (and shouting
woooo-hooooooo as you went!)?

Or, as I mention in chapter 2, maybe you've wished you had a
sword like She-Ra's, which could turn you into a superhuman
version of yourself? Not to mention gift you a talking unicorn too.
I've definitely wished for all three — and lots more besides!

In fact, whenever I saw or read about anything I considered
a superpower on TV or in a book, I would promptly start
daydreaming and imagining what it would be like to have the
exact same powers as the character I was watching or reading
about. Whether it was reading Roald Dahl's *The Wonderful Story of
Henry Sugar* or *Matilda* (in both of which the main characters use
their minds and eyes as a superpower — something that led me
to run home and try and move things with my mind for hours on

end. Safe to say, that did NOT work . . .) or watching *The Teenage Mutant Ninja Turtles* (a show about four turtles who fight crime after a radioactive chemical spill falls on them and gives them human strengths) and wondering how I could develop extra-fast reflexes (especially as I was always spilling things!), I think I spent pretty much most of my life imagining what it might be like to be someone else. Especially if that someone else was fictional.

Reflection

Who is your most favourite super-heroic character that you have ever read about or watched? If you could pick one of their powers for yourself, what would it be and what would you do with it?

Another character that I absolutely could not get enough of, when I was around eight, used to drop in via my TV set every Saturday afternoon. Except, unlike most of my favourite programmes, this character wasn't in a cartoon — it was an action series with real people acting in it and performing epic stunts. The main character was an Amazonian woman called Diana, who, much like Superman or She-Ra, lives a double life: one as a seemingly ordinary woman and the other as Wonder Woman — a fighter against all types of cruel villains.

Wonder Woman has three things that helped her fight villains:

1. A whip called the 'Lasso of Truth', which can make anyone tied up with it tell the truth

2. A tiara that serves as a flying disc, which she can throw to cut through things or stop people

3. A pair of indestructible bracelets that can deflect anything — from bullets to any kind of force that is trying to hurt her

ALL AWESOME TOOLS TO HAVE!

But there was one of these in particular that all my friends at school and I used to pretend we could have for ourselves — and that was, of course, those bracelets. In the show, they looked like golden shirt cuffs with a red star on them. Easy enough to make with a bit of paper, a pair of scissors, a red pen and some sticky tape. So that is exactly what we did when we had those things to hand, and when we didn't, we just used our imagination. By simply crossing our wrists to make an 'X', we would push away the imaginary weapons our friends were trying to throw at us, and we would imagine fighting off evil wherever we found it. Some of my best memories are of us sprinting down the corridors of the flat I lived in or running round and round in circles in the school playground, doing just that!

Wonder Woman's ability to deflect anything that might hurt her (making it change direction) is something that still fascinates me to this day. And the more birthdays that have passed, the more and more I have come to realise that the ability to do just that — to spot a harmful thing and deflect it away from you — is a skill that we *all* need. Especially in a world where there are lots of people who may not be truthful about who they are or who may be using their platforms to make fun of people or bully them.

Reflection

TIPS ON HOW TO DEFLECT NEGATIVE FORCES

We may not all have access to Wonder Woman's bracelets, but that doesn't mean we can't deflect bad energies that are trying to hurt us. Here are my top tips on how to spot and push away those negative energies:

1. Identify anything around you that makes you feel fidgety, anxious or unhappy. It might be a messy bedroom. Or a friend who makes you feel bad about yourself. Or not feeling satisfied with your grades at school. Whatever it is, spot it and then work on fixing it. You have the power to build the kind of world you want to live in. And it starts with you knowing what works for you and what doesn't, and changing the things that definitely don't work and which make you unhappy.

2. If you hear people saying things about you, your ideas or the things you care about that aren't true or are hurtful, breathe in for five seconds and then out for ten. Then mentally throw the comments you have just

heard as far away from you
as you can. Imagine them being sucked into
a black hole or being thrown out into the depths of space.

Pushing negative, hurtful comments away from our minds
is something lots of activists have to do nearly every day to
preserve their energy for what matters most. Because sadly,
there are lots of people who are hurt or angry or scared
themselves and want to take their frustrations out on others;
or who don't have enough empathy, kindness, patience or
respect for others who may want and need different things,
or come from different backgrounds and experiences. But if
those comments are so hurtful or violent that they scare you
or can't be pushed away, it is important you report them to a
grown-up you trust immediately so that action against anyone
trying to bully you can be taken.

3. Do you ever notice yourself complaining about something
over and over again? What is it you're complaining about and
why are you complaining about it? Make a tally of the number
of times you complain in a week: it's important to know.

WHY?

Well, because the more negative signals and words you send back to your brain, the more likely you will feel upset and down and channel all that negative energy into what you do. It's like an Olympic trainer shouting at their team and telling them that they're rubbish all the time. And the more they do it and the louder they shout, the worse the Olympic athletes feel and the worse they perform. How awful would that be?

Similarly, your way of thinking and the words you use for yourself can impact your day and the way you feel — and the way others around you feel too. And the last thing you want is to be the one responsible for creating negative energy that sucks your own force fields dry! So identify your complaints and replace each one with something to be grateful for. I promise you, having been a HUGE complainer when I was at school (mainly over things my little brother did and homework!), shifting the way you think and making something negative into something positive can make a lifelong difference to your energy levels and how hopeful you feel about things.

Let's try it . . . For example, one of the things I am always complaining about is not being able to finish all the things I wanted to get done in a single day. It makes me incredibly upset knowing that there are things I need to do that I just can't get to.

So whenever I do get upset, instead I write out all the things I DID do — including all the extra things I wasn't expecting to do (like running to the post office or helping out a friend). It completely flips my day around, makes me feel instantly better and leaves me feeling incredibly grateful.

It is so important that we take care of ourselves and have time-outs when we need to, so that we can stay sharp and focused and filled with the energy we need to get on with our goals. There is nothing worse than trying to do something when you are too tired to do it properly, and as the world needs you and your voice, we also need you to make sure that you take care of it by taking care of yourself. And the best thing is, it's not a hard thing to do at all! Because all you really have to do is schedule in breaks that will help you help you forge your three Rs:

REST, REFLECT AND REJUVENATE.

Reflection

REST, REFLECT AND REJUVENATE: WHAT ARE YOUR THREE RS?

1. **REST:** What is your favourite way of resting? (And yes, reading a comic book upside down on your bed counts!)

2. **REFLECT:** What do you like to do after something wonderful has happened (such as having a super fun Christmas or Eid or Hannukah or Diwali, getting a great grade for a piece of homework that you weren't expecting or getting a part in the school assembly that you had been wanting)? Do you write a diary? Do you like to just stare up at the ceiling and have A Very Long Think? Or maybe you like to tell your mum or dad or carer all about it and love seeing their reactions? Doing whatever gives you time to think over something that has just happened — whether it was a happy event or a sad one — is sure to be just what you need.

3. **REJUVENATE:** To rejuvenate means to gather up new energy. Think of it as recharging the batteries in a torch after the light has been left on for a long time.

What kind of things do you like to do to fill yourself up with new energy and get excited for the next challenge ahead? (For me, after Something Big has happened — such as finishing writing this chapter! — I like to close my eyes for a few seconds to think on it, make myself a huge cup of tea, watch something incredibly funny or go for a walk. Doing this will help me think of the next writing adventure I want to have. All simple things, but all of which make me relax.)

At school and right through to university, whenever there was a big exam, I would get so nervous that I would forget to eat, drink or even sleep properly! All things that I still do when I'm working on a project that I'm passionate about. So the three Rs are an area that I have to work on all the time, and which I know a lot of people passionate about their work struggle with too, whether they're an artist or an activist or the leader of a country!

But I'm always keen to learn from others and have picked up lots of tips and tricks from activists who are really good at persevering their energy and strengthening their force fields. And all of them are different and unique.

For example, no matter how busy he used to get, former US president Barack Obama would go and catch a game of basketball to re-energise himself. Michelle Obama, the former first lady, loved to listen to music and go for a bike ride.

Poet, writer, activist and director Maya Angelou used to take long, hot baths to think of her next story or article (a fact which led to bath bombs being named after her!), whilst actress and UNHCR ambassador Angelina Jolie likes to hit the trampoline or do some colouring in. Activist Malcolm X used to head straight for a local library to read just as much as he could in a day. Singer Ed Sheeran likes to make things with LEGO and play Monopoly. And even the Queen likes to go for walks or play with her pet corgis every day, or go on breaks to the countryside with her family — even if it means having to work whilst she is away with them.

No matter how much they had or have to do, or how important their goals, each of these incredibly famous people always set aside time to stop and do the things that strengthen their own personal force fields before they continue in their goals. In other words, they plan and take the time for self-care by actively doing something to make themselves happy and healthy and to take time away from stresses and anxieties.

And if *they* can do it, so can we! So arm yourself with the things that make you truly happy, cross those wrists and protect your time and energy from all negative forces.

SUGGESTIONS FOR YOUR SELF-CARE ROUTINE

Self-care isn't just a once-in-a-while thing. Every single one of us needs to practise a little self-care and self-appreciation every single day! Try and see if you can make the following actions a part of your every day, even in the middle of all your chores and homework and clubs and school!

1. On the days you're not running late for school, take exactly one minute (you can even time it if you like) to sit on the floor or on your bed, close your eyes, breathe in and out deeply and think about . . . absolutely nothing! Clear your mind of all the things that normally clutter your brain from the moment you wake up, and try to silence your thoughts. Switching off the brain like this is a brilliant way of calming the day — and your body — down before it all kicks off, and the moment you open your eyes and switch on again, you will feel more energised!

2. Whenever you're brushing your teeth or combing (or gelling up!) your hair, SLOOOOOOOOOOOOOW it right down. Take a few extra seconds for each thing, really enjoy what you're doing to take care of your body and think about how amazing everything you have is — from your skin to the way things feel to your teeth and hair and eyebrows and lips and nose . . . It's all pretty awesome, so take a few moments to recognise what you have and pamper it all!

3. No matter how good or bad your day is, be sure to stop and take a break in the middle of it all. It's why we have lunchtimes, after all! So whether it's heading out for a game of basketball or football (or football-rounders!) in the playground with all your best friends, or having lunch with your family (even if they're super weird and annoying), or staring out of the window to have a good ol' daydream, or picking up a book to have just a dip of a read, take A Proper Break. It can feel like a mini-holiday for your mind and body, and it will let you get back to the second half of the day with gusto!

4. Do one thing you love every day. It could be inventing your own story, humming a tune, watching an episode of your favourite cartoon, doing cartwheels in the park or your garden, bugging your mum or dad or foster carer with questions, having a bit of chocolate, building LEGO, colouring in or making a puzzle. Whatever it might be, if you possibly can, do it, even if only for a few seconds, every day.

5. At the end of the day, your brain will be full of new ideas and thoughts and possibly even worries about what it needs to do or should have done or wishes it could do. The best way to calm it is to get it all out! So whether you call it a Captain's Log, a Diary, a To-Do List or The Records of My Awesome Brain, write out your thoughts, make a list of what you want to do the next day and try to free up your mind for all those dreams it needs to have. Writing thoughts out on paper is like creating a download centre and back-up drive for your brain all in one go. And as well as shifting all those things you're holding inside of you to the outside so that you feel lighter, it will help you remember things better too — because you'll have written it all out.

6. Just before you go to sleep, say out loud (or whisper it if you share a room) three things that happened in the day that made you feel happy, or three things you feel grateful for.

And if you're already making time in your day to do the things you love and which don't involve working (or worrying about working), then your force fields are likely to be of the very best kind: totally off the charts!

RE-ENERGISING YOUR FORCE FIELDS

1. It's important to know that with each goal accomplished (even the seemingly small ones!) or piece of homework finished, there is a treat that is awaiting you. (Mine tends to be a movie or an art exhibition I haven't seen yet. Or a LEGO set I want to buy and build. Or a book I want to read — with a big cup of tea and some chocolate to hand, of course.) Think of the next big piece of work you have to do — or a goal you want to accomplish — and then think of the treat you are going to give yourself when you complete it.

2. What are the five things you love to do most in the world, either at home or at school? List them in order of the joy they bring you (and yes, this CAN include sleeping!).

3. *** STAR ACTION ***

Create your own timeline of joy. Pull out your diary or grab your notepad and write down five dates in the coming weeks when you will get to do each of the things you have listed in the question above.

THE AWARD FOR 'CHAMPION FORCE-FIELD PROTECTOR' GOES TO . . .

NAME: **ADELE**

ROLE: **MULTI-AWARD-WINNING SINGER**

CHAMPION FORCE-FIELD PROTECTOR

Adele is one of the world's bestselling music artists. From Oscars to BRIT Awards and Golden Globes to multiple Grammy Awards, she has won every award anyone could ever wish to win, has topped global charts and achieved world records with every single and album she has released, and is considered one of the most successful female musicians in history.

But this fact that doesn't stop her from disappearing from the limelight and taking a step back from being famous for five or even six years at a time!

By not pushing herself to constantly create new material, enjoying time in private with her loved ones and taking care of her voice, Adele ensures that she can gather both new material for potential songs and the strength she needs to produce the very best work and perform at concerts around the world.
Her self-care not only enables her to continue creating and singing songs that are loved by the whole world, but helps ensure she can continue to support the many, many charities she donates to. These charities include Sands (which supports parents whose children have sadly died), drop4drop (which develops clean water solutions across the world) and MusiCares (which helps musicians in need) amongst many, many others. Adele is proof that taking time out when you need to, and stepping back from endless cycles of work, is nothing but a brilliant thing to do.

Chapter 10

ARISE! BEARER OF EXCALIBUR:

WHY HOPE REALLY IS ON THE HORIZON

unique

Being the only one of its kind. Being unlike anything else.

YOU DID IT!
YOU'VE MADE IT ALL THE WAY HERE!

To the very last chapter . . . (And yup, this celebration still counts even if you've skipped everything else and jumped straight to this page!)

I hope you're feeling as excited as I am. Because just think of it! In a few pages' time, you'll be closing this book and off you'll go, like a knight or a knightess in shining armour, to continue your own explorations, adventures and quests. If that doesn't make your insides go slightly giddy with anticipation, then I don't know what will!

Gosh . . . I wish I could reach through the pages of this book and gift you something to mark the end of our journey together. Like a royal velvet cloak to help keep you warm on the adventure ahead (and to make you look super cool too) . . .

Or a crown (not a huge one, just one that is perfectly suited to you and your head) to put on whenever you feel as if the quest you're on is getting too hard and you could use a reminder that the people of your worlds need you . . .

OOOOOH! Or a sword . . . But not just any old sword! A sword designed only for you, crafted and made up of all your best strengths so that no one else *but* you can use it.

HOLD ON . . .

Wait a cloud-floating minute! Now that my imagination has you dressed in a cloak and a crown and given you a sword, you definitely look like . . . Yes, you do! Like a completely you-version of King Arthur holding up Excalibur!

Well! I don't mind telling you that THAT has made *me* go slightly giddy and tingly too! Because I *loved* the legend of King Arthur when I was at school. I couldn't get enough of the stories, all of which have stuck with me and which pop up in my memories at very special moments like this one.

Can *you* remember the first time you ever heard of the legend of King Arthur? (If THIS is actually the very first time you've ever heard of him or his sword, Excalibur, and you are wondering what on earth is happening, then please put this book down IMMEDIATELY and go and ask all the grown-ups of your world: (a) why on earth they've been hiding such a great story away from you, and (b) to tell you as much about King Arthur as they can.)

I can remember when I first heard it super clearly, because it was one of the best story-sharing moments I ever had.

It was in school, when I was around eight years old, on what I remember being a brilliantly bright morning. Mrs Koumi (favourite teacher on the planet) made everyone in my class put down our pencils and close up our workbooks, as she picked up what looked like a big, fat history textbook from her (constantly messy) table.

But it wasn't a history textbook at all. It was a giant book stamped with the words 'THE ARTHURIAN LEGENDS' on its cover, above a painting of a man wearing a crown, lying down on the floor as if he were sleeping, and surrounded by women in long robes who seemed to be crying for him.

And as Mrs Koumi began to read and unveil the legend of King Arthur with each page, the more and more fascinated I became. After all, King Arthur was no ordinary mythical king. He was a king who, as one version of the legend goes, started life as an orphan boy, living at a time when Britain had no king to lead it, which meant that the whole country was falling into greed and darkness. And it was *this* orphan boy who, at the age of just ten, went on to claim the sword Excalibur: a sword whose blade had been stuck in a huge rock for years and years, and which even the strongest men in the country couldn't pull out. No matter how hard they tried, they didn't possess what Arthur had — which was the most courageous and worthiest of hearts — a heart worthy of a king. The sword belonged to him and him alone, no matter who else tried to claim it, and ultimately it revealed his true destiny to the world. A destiny that would involve creating the Round Table — a table around which only the most noble, trusted and wisest of knights could sit, and where they would be treated as equals not only with each other, but with the king too.

Imagine being SO courageous and SO worthy and deserving that you got to claim the throne of your country when you were still young enough to be at school!

Reflection

If you found out that **YOU** were the king or queen of a country right this minute:

1. What one action would you take immediately?

2. WHICH OF YOUR TWO QUALITIES (iN OTHER WORDS, THE TWO VERY BEST THINGS ABOUT YOURSELF) WOULD YOU USE TO HELP ALL THE PEOPLE OF YOUR LAND?

3. Name 10 people you would invite to be the Knights of your Round Table to help you govern your country. (They can be people you already know or who you don't know but admire. And yup! They can be from the present or from way back in history!) Why have you picked them?

In T.H White's version of the Arthurian legends, which began with the book *The Sword in the Stone* (later made into a Disney cartoon film of the exact same name, which I still love watching to this day), Arthur doesn't even have a name and is called 'The Wart' (how horrible and yucky is that? Warts are gross!). He is also treated as a servant by his selfish, show-off older adopted brother, Kay. In short, he is very much a character who could have been bitter and angry and mean because of all the terrible things he goes through. But he chooses not to be, which is a running theme with a great many of the world's kindest and wisest of leaders.

There is, of course, one person who knows exactly who Arthur was always destined to be. And that is none other than someone who may very well be the original wizard, Merlin, who steps in to train Arthur for his kingship — largely by turning him into all kinds of animals to help him see the world from different perspectives!

Reflection

If you could choose a creature to be turned into for a day, what would you want to be, and why? What do you think you would learn from the experience that you could use to help others? (I would choose to be a Bengal tiger because sadly, there are now so few of them left in the world that they are at risk of becoming extinct. I would want to be one not just because of their amazing fiery orange and black striped coats, but to learn what it must be like for them trying to escape human beings who want to poach and hunt them.)

Together, Merlin and Arthur may have been the first ever boy-wizard team in English mythical history (long before J.K. Rowling's Harry Potter and Dumbledore duo magically entered our lives). And it's a team that has survived thousands of years of storytelling and goes on capturing imaginations the world over. Largely because at its heart is a friendship in which someone young is learning from someone far older and wiser — which is something we all do if we're lucky enough. Whether it's listening to our parents or guardians, hearing our grandparents or grand-aunts and -uncles tell stories (even if they are really weird and we can't understand why they find themselves funny!) or paying attention to our teachers at school (yup, even in the lessons we can't wait to be over!), we're surrounded by older, wiser people. The gift of being allowed to learn from someone who has lived in the world much longer than us, and who wants to pass on their teachings to us, is something that no clever person would ever turn down. (And yup, I know parents, teachers and older brothers and sisters and cousins can be super annoying. But even they sometimes have some really cool knowledge. I promise!)

At school, I didn't really care that King Arthur was the stuff of legendary fiction (or was he? Did you know that some historians believe the stories were created by people wanting to honour a real-life leader and hero of the sixth century? And that there is evidence that King Arthur may have been a real person?). His legend and stories *felt* to me as if they could be real. And what's more, Arthur seemed like a boy who, if he had been real and walked into my class one day, I would definitely have wanted to hang out with!

Luckily, lots of my friends in class felt the same. So within days of learning all we could about him from Mrs Koumi, we all stopped playing our usual games of tag or seeing who could do a handstand the longest, and began galloping around at speed on make-believe horses and holding the kind of duels we imagined King Arthur and his knights might have fought (cue lots of arguments in the playground over whose turn it was to be King Arthur, and whether spoons smuggled out of the dinner hall counted as swords!).

The idea that someone seemingly small and ordinary, and who was even bullied and treated horribly, could actually possess great power, wisdom and courage, is a timeless and much-loved one.

It's why so many of the greatest s/heroes of both the real world and fictional stories fit what I call I Arthur Mould. And I think it's why poets, storytellers and artists continue to speak of, draw, sing, write and make films about characters who, even before they become the great leader or s/hero they are destined to be, share the exact same characteristics Arthur had before he became king — characteristics he had when he was a boy, and which included:

1. Being kind and caring – even when others weren't kind or caring to him

2. Having empathy for others – including animals and the natural world

3. Being honest – even when that honesty got him into trouble in the short term

4. Being brave – especially when it came to helping others

5. Putting others first – in the legend, Arthur doesn't pull the sword Excalibur for himself – he takes it to help his adopted brother, Kay (yup! The mean, horrible one!). He doesn't think of himself at all and just wants to help out.

6. Forgiveness – Arthur is always forgiving Kay! (Did I mention he was mean and horrible?!)

7. Always wanting to listen to and learn from others – not just Merlin, but his adopted father and anyone else who can teach him something

8. Being passionate about fairness and justice

All these qualities are traits that we've looked at throughout this book, and together they make the child Arthur a leader-in-waiting from the very beginning of the story. He might not see it, but he is worthy of grasping and raising the sword Excalibur, even when he is so young, because he possesses the very qualities and gifts the world desperately needs more of.

When I look at all the amazing activists I get to meet and work with every day, it doesn't surprise me in the least that Arthur's destiny is revealed to him at such a young age. Because whenever I get to learn more about the people I work with and find out when it was they first started wanting to help people, guess what? ALL of them turn out to be hidden King Arthurs who began their work when they were still at school.

Reflection

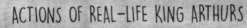

ACTIONS OF REAL—LIFE KING ARTHURS

These are just some of the things lots of the activists I work with did when they were at school — and which you can definitely do too! Things like . . .

* Taking part in a charity cake sale

* Saving up lunch or birthday money to buy something for someone or donating it to a local charity

* Using pocket money to sponsor an animal or plant a tree

* Doing a fun run to raise money for a charity

* Helping out a friend with their homework

* Donating toys to Christmas appeals or to the local hospital

Getting petitions signed by everyone in class

 Helping a neighbour

Writing letters and Christmas cards for people being looked after by local homeless charities

 Donating food for local charities

Taking care of your grandparents

Doing a recycling drive

Babysitting brothers and sisters

Writing thank-you cards to nurses and doctors

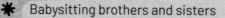

The activists I know all did things for other people and continued doing them, and doing them, and doing them, until . . . That was it! They just couldn't stop, and they knew that helping others or campaigning for a particular cause was all they wanted to do!

One such real-life King Arthur of my world is Caroline Cottet. And I want to finish off this chapter and this book by telling you a little bit about her, because I think she is one of the most special, secretly royal people to exist on the planet.

And I don't think she has just one Excalibur in her world — I think she must have at least fifty! All pulled out whilst she was still in school — even though she didn't know it!

Caroline has been working in the refugee camps of northern France since 2015. Many people would never know on meeting her that she is the quiet, secret force behind much of the best and kindest work taking place in the refugee camps of Calais and Dunkirk in France and beyond. She doesn't wear a cloak or a crown (although I think she should!), but she does what King Arthur did so brilliantly: she unites people around lots of different round tables so that they can all work together and listen to each other in order to help refugees in the best way possible.

Behind Caroline's wonderful grin is a woman who helped co-found the Refugee Women's Centre: the only organisation on the ground which helps women and families specifically. Not only that, she also founded Maison Sesame, a very special welcoming house where refugees who are especially ill and frightened can be looked after in a real house, surrounded by a beautiful garden. And as if those two things weren't huge enough, Caroline is also the Field Director for O's Refugee Aid Team — my team! And through her work with us, she helps lots of refugee charities to survive and grow, whilst even taking refugee families into her own home to make sure they stay safe and have food and shelter.

At school, Caroline says she didn't really do anything big to help anyone. She 'only' helped a friend one day by letting her borrow her watch. And she 'only' helped her family to raise funds or do work for their chosen charities when they asked her to. And she 'only' tried to be nice to everyone in her class because she wanted everyone to get on and be nice to her and each other.

All things she thought weren't big actions, but which would have seemed like huge, wonderful actions to everyone she did help. And which, I have absolutely no doubt in my mind, led her to become the leader she is today. Complete with an invisible crown, cloak and sword — just like yours . . .

REMEMBER YOUR LEGENDARY POWERS

Here we are, at the final call to action. And it's going to end with where we started: Y O U

WONDERFUL, UNIQUE AND POWERFUL YOU.

The you that no one else can ever copy — no matter how clever they might be!

The you as special and as distinctive as your DNA.

And as you leave me and these words behind, please don't forget to call on your powers every day and wherever you can. Your powers to:

1. *** STAR ACTION ***

Be kind to everyone you meet — even to those who might not seem very nice or might be bullies because they themselves need help or are hurt.

2. Care, and care deeply, about the things that matter to you — the fact you care about them is what makes you Rather Wonderful.

3. Start discussions at home and in class about the things you want to know more about. Remember, don't be afraid to ask your questions and be your own private detective. The only person who can get up to go and seek answers to your questions is you.

4. Join in with the amazing things that are already happening in the world. There are already incredible groups and movements championing all the issues you care about so join up, volunteer and help raise awareness or funds or do both. Your voice is what matters, and it is not alone. You have the power to add it to whatever cause you feel strongly about.

5. Call on the grown—ups of your world to listen to you — no matter how powerful they might think themselves or how many titles they hold.

6. Learn just as much as you can about the very best things and ways to be.

7. Come up with new ideas, new ways of seeing a problem and new solutions for the issues that are worrying you.

8. Never forget your ripple effects and just how eternal and powerful they are.

9. Take care of the people you love — and yourself too — so you can go on to do great things together.

10. Become the kind of person you wish others would be — and the world needs.

All these powers you hold, right now, literally at your fingertips, make you incredibly special and powerful. After all, you have within you the capacity to change things for the better every single day of your life, and to make everyone in your world feel hope in all the things you will go on to do.

My hope for you is that you *never* lose sight of this fact, or the fact YOU are It. YOU are the world's hope on the horizon. Your cares, your passions, your actions and everything that makes you the very best version of you that you can be will forge the hopes for better, kinder days ahead for all who know you. And should you ever feel lost or worried or anxious about anything happening in the world, I want you to head straight to a mirror, look into your own wondrous eyes and repeat the words:

i AM HOPE ON THE HORiZON.
i AM NOT ALONE.
AND i AM RiSiNG.

Because hope really is everywhere. All we have to do is remember it lives on in all of us.

And if that isn't reason enough to grab a piece of chocolate* and celebrate, then I know nothing . . .

*41: the number of times I've managed to say 'chocolate' in this book. Yum.

THE AWARD FOR BEING 'MOST LIKELY TO BECOME A LEGEND' GOES TO . . .

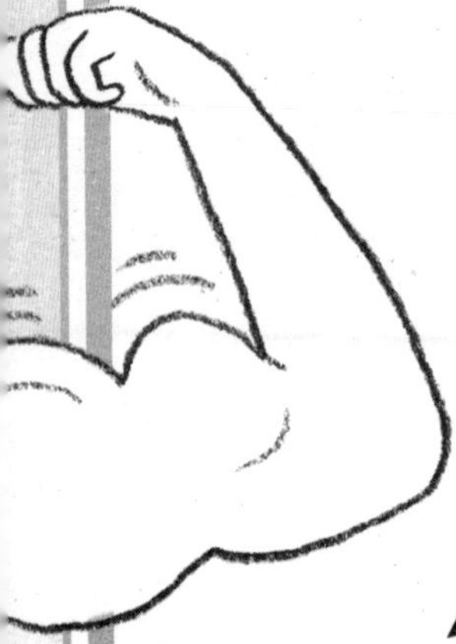

YOU

Because you're here, having read all the words that came before these ones.

Because you've already been making your legendary mark on the world and the people in it, just by being alive and being who you are.

And because every good and wonderful hope you hold for yourself is the exact hope the world holds for you too and needs to see come to fruition.

So arise, noble heart, and go forth! Know that your every action and every intention, matters to us all.

AND THANK YOU.

For making your mark on me too, by having picked up this book and allowing me to be a part of your journey.

And for gifting me the hope I needed, that the world is going to be a more beautiful, kind and compassionate one, thanks to *you* . . .

HOPE ON THE HORIZON
READING AND VIEWING LIST

READiNG LiST

✳ *Charlie and the Chocolate Factory* by Roald Dahl

✳ *No One Is Too Small to Make a Difference* by Greta Thunberg

✳ *Norse Myths: Tales of Odin, Thor and Loki* by
   Kevin Crossley-Holland

✳ *A Picture Book of Frederick Douglass* by David A. Adler,
   illustrated by Samuel Byrd

✳ *I Am Malala* by Malala Yousafzai and Christina Lamb

✳ *Albert Einstein (Little People, BIG DREAMS series)* by Maria
   Isabel Sanchez Vegara, illustrated by Jean Claude

✳ *The Adventures of Tintin: The Castafiore Emerald;
   Cigars of the Pharoah; Land of Black Gold; Tintin in Tibet*
   by Hergé

✳ *The Famous Five: Five on a Treasure Island* by Enid Blyton

✳ *Work It, Girl: Oprah Winfrey: Run the show like CEO*
   by Caroline Moss, illustrated by Sinem Erkas

✳ *The Railway Children* by E. Nesbit

✳ *The Adventures of Sherlock Holmes* by Arthur Conan Doyle

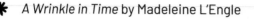

* *A Wrinkle in Time* by Madeleine L'Engle

* *Nelson Mandela: Long Walk to Freedom* by Chris Van Wyk and Nelson Mandela, illustrated by Paddy Bouma

* *The Wizard of Oz* by L. Frank Baum

* *Human Computer: Mary Jackson, Engineer* by Andi Diehn and Katie Mazeika

* *The Lion, the Witch and the Wardrobe* by C.S. Lewis

* *To Kill a Mockingbird* by Harper Lee

* *Life Doesn't Frighten Me* by Maya Angelou

* *Kofi and His Magic* by Maya Angelou

* *The Seed of Compassion* by His Holiness Dalai Lama, illustrated by Bao Luu

* *Coat of Many Colors* by Dolly Parton, illustrated by Brooke Boynton-Hughes

* *The Star Outside My Window* by . . . me! (That's me as in Onjali Raúf, not 'me' as in the name of another author. Although, how cool would it be to be called 'Me' and write 'by Me' everywhere!)

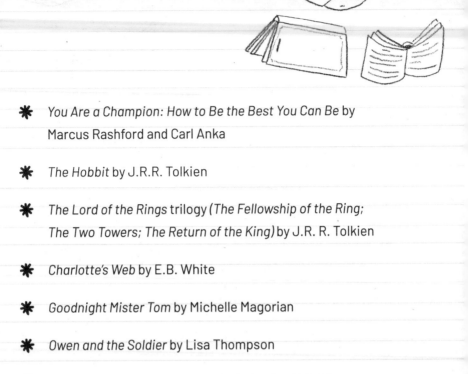

* *You Are a Champion: How to Be the Best You Can Be* by Marcus Rashford and Carl Anka

* *The Hobbit* by J.R.R. Tolkien

* *The Lord of the Rings* trilogy (*The Fellowship of the Ring; The Two Towers; The Return of the King*) by J.R. R. Tolkien

* *Charlotte's Web* by E.B. White

* *Goodnight Mister Tom* by Michelle Magorian

* *Owen and the Soldier* by Lisa Thompson

* *The Wonderful Story of Henry Sugar* by Roald Dahl

* *Matilda* by Roald Dahl

* *Know Your Rights: and Claim Them* by Angelina Jolie, Amnesty International and Geraldine Van Bueren

* *The Story of King Arthur and His Knights* by Howard Pyle

* *The Sword in the Stone* by T. H. White

* *Harry Potter and The Philosopher's Stone* by J.K. Rowling

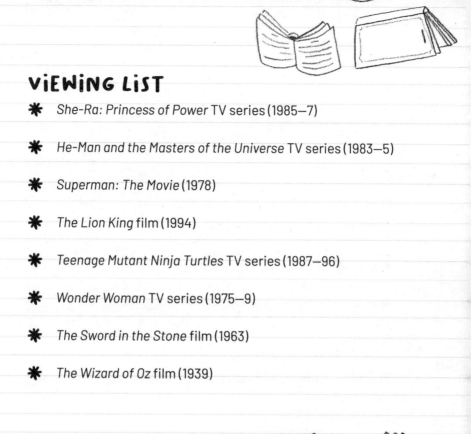

ViEWiNG LiST

* *She-Ra: Princess of Power* TV series (1985–7)

* *He-Man and the Masters of the Universe* TV series (1983–5)

* *Superman: The Movie* (1978)

* *The Lion King* film (1994)

* *Teenage Mutant Ninja Turtles* TV series (1987–96)

* *Wonder Woman* TV series (1975–9)

* *The Sword in the Stone* film (1963)

* *The Wizard of Oz* film (1939)

GLOSSARY

* **activist:** Someone who deeply cares about making a difference and campaigns to change things for the better.

* **apartheid:** A system of keeping people apart or treating them unjustly on the grounds of their race.

* **child food poverty:** Children who are not able to access the food supplies they need to function on a day-to-day basis and who, as a result, suffer from long-term and consistent hunger. Families of children who live in conditions of poverty may also be sacrificing food allowances to pay for heating, lighting, shelter, clothes and the other basic things we all need to survive.

* **climate change:** A long-term change in the average temperatures/weather patterns across the earth's local, regional and global climates. The most negative climate change caused by human-produced temperature increases (otherwise known as global warming) is the result of increased levels of carbon dioxide, caused by the use of fossil fuels and the destruction of forests and other natural climates.

* **discrimination:** Treating someone unjustly, differently or even horribly because of their race, age, sex, disability or any other perceived difference.

✻ **feminist:** Someone who believes men and women should be treated equally in all aspects of life.

✻ **food bank:** A place where people can receive food, basic toiletries and other forms of help, free of charge, if they are struggling with food poverty. There are thousands of food banks operating from warehouses, churches, mosques, synagogues and even schools across the UK, with lots of people donating to them every day — including supermarkets, bakeries and restaurants.

✻ **free school meals:** Meals which are given at school to children whose families are on low incomes and need government help to survive (I used to be a free school meals kid sometimes when I was at school!).

✻ **humanitarian:** Someone who cares about, and who tries to help, the welfare, health and happiness of other people.

✻ **humility:** The quality of never ever thinking you are better or more important than other people.

✻ **injustice:** A wrong or unfair act which hurts the rights of other people.

✳ **Nazis:** People who follow(ed) the far-right, extreme terrorist and racist views held by Hitler and the National Socialist German Workers' Party (the Nazi party), who rose to power in the 1920s and were defeated by defeated by all the countries who joined together to fight against them in the Second World War.

✳ **NHS:** The National Health Service, which runs all free medical services such as doctors' surgeries and hospitals across the United Kingdom.

✳ **Nobel Prize:** An award given out to recognise achievements or creations in six key areas that have helped all of humankind. The six international Nobel prize categories are physics, chemistry, medicine, literature, economics and the promotion of peace.

✳ **oratory:** An ability to speak publicly in an eloquent, formal, expressive and persuasive manner.

✳ **philanthropist:** Someone who likes to support good causes and help others, usually by donating money.

✳ **racism:** Treating a person differently or unfairly because of their skin colour, religious faith or cultural background.

* **refuge:** A place which provides safety or shelter to someone in need or in danger.

* **refugee:** A person who has been forced to leave their home, town and sometimes even their country in order to escape war, persecution or natural disasters like those triggered by climate change.

* **refugee rights:** Every refugee has the right to seek safety (asylum) in a new part of the world when in their lives are in danger and to be given the same rights as the citizens of the country they are seeking safety in — including freedom of thought, freedom of movement and freedom from torture and degrading treatment.

* **revolution:** Forcefully removing a government or a structure of power, in favour of a new system.

* **segregation:** Placing someone or something apart from others and treating them unjustly and differently.

* **sexism:** Treating a person differently and unfairly because of their sex or gender.

* **women's rights:** Rights that promote the legal, political and social equality of women to be the same as that of men.

* **First World War:** A global war that began in 1914 after the assassination of Archduke Franz Ferdinand of Austria and lasted until 1918, during which at least 16 million people — including civilians — from all over the world were killed. After the war, the leaders of the major winning countries (the USA, France, Britain and Italy) created an agreement called the Treaty of Versailles to punish Germany for their actions in the war: a decision that tragically led to events which would ultimately launch the Second World War.

* **Second World War:** A global war that lasted from 1939 to 1945, which sought to end the rise of Nazism and fascism, and was started by Hitler's violent and racist ruling policies as the leader of Germany and his attempted invasion of different countries across the world.

RESOURCES AND LINKS TO CHARITY ORGANISATIONS

CHAPTER 1

✳ **Mobile Refugee Support** www.mobilerefugeesupport.org

✳ **UNHCR statistics** www.unhcr.org/refugee-statistics

✳ **The Year of Greta** www.theyearofgreta.com

CHAPTER 2

✳ **UNICEF – Girls' education**
www.unicef.org/education/girls-education

✳ **Lola's Homeless**
www.facebook.com/groups/LolasHomeless

✳ **Childline (UK)** www.childline.org.uk

✳ **Kids Helpline (Australia)** www.kidshelpline.com.au

✳ **headspace (Australia)** www.headspace.org.au

✳ **Youthline (New Zealand)** www.youthline.co.nz

CHAPTER 3

✳ **Buses 4 Homeless** www.buses4homeless.org

✳ **International Rescue Committee** www.rescue-uk.org

CHAPTER 4

✳ **Refugee Biryani and Bananas**

www.refugeebiriyanibananas.org

✳ **Oprah Winfrey Charitable Foundation**

www.oprahfoundation.org

CHAPTER 5

✳ **Anti-Slavery International**

www.antislavery.org/slavery-today

✳ **The Voice of Domestic Workers**

www.thevoiceofdomesticworkers.com

✳ **Nelson Mandela Foundation** www.nelsonmandela.org

CHAPTER 6

✳ **Women in STEM** www.womeninstem.co.uk

CHAPTER 7
* **Children's Society** www.childrenssociety.org.uk

* **Making Herstory** www.makingherstory.org.uk

* **#ENDCHILDFOODPOVERTY** www.endchildfoodpoverty.org

* **Trussell Trust** www.trusselltrust.org

CHAPTER 8
* **The LemonAid Boys** www.facebook.com/theLemonAidboys

CHAPTER 9
* **Sands** www.sands.org.uk

* **Drop4Drop** www.drop4drop.org

* **MusiCares** www.musicares.org

CHAPTER 10
* **O's Refugee Aid Team** www.osrefugeeaidteam.org

ACKNOWLEDGEMENTS

Pulling together all the delicious strands needed for this book, centred on people and matters so close to my heart, and written for an audience so utterly epic in every single way, has been such a joy and a pleasure that I can barely believe I got to do it. Never did I think that I would be able to take the time to ponder on the most inspirational stories and characters and real-life s/heroes who have made such an impact on me – whether they landed in my universe via a story book, the playground, the TV set or in the midst of my most recent works – as 'work'. But I did and do, and for this honour, I have a world of people to thank . . .

First and foremost, the most important people on Planet Earth to thank for this book not only coming into being, but even being proposed in the first place, has to go to you: dear reader extraordinaire . . . It was solely thanks to you and your staggering abilities to read the other book babies, take away the messages you did, and then self-mobilise to help others in ways unfathomed, that triggered the idea for this non-fiction book in the first place (I really do mean it when I say each of you deserves a crown and a cloak, and that your actions have shifted and changed my worlds too!).

Next, I can't help but send extra-long, eternal hugs to my editors and compilers at Wren & Rook, who made these pages come together like patchwork pieces to become a book-quilt. My deepest gratitude to you, dearest Laura Horsley, Kaltoun Yusuf and Victoria Walsh for orchestrating this project so magnificently, and for bearing with me so patiently whilst I disappeared and reappeared and disappeared again as is my wont. And Kat Slack, designer supreme: thank you for fitting what I thought might be Way (Waaaaaay!) Too Much Text, and forging a layout that feels like a hundred pieces of floating artworks come together. Only a true designing magician could have accomplished this so swiftly as you have done! I have loved working with you all: thank you for making it so ridiculously easy, and for each of your kindnesses every step of the way. What a dream-team you have been!

Silvia Molteni, despite being away for the duration of this book's creation to take care of beautiful blossoming hopes of your own, this whole project would not have been birthed without you. Thank you for always setting to paper such incredible visions I would never dare have for myself, and making them real somehow. I am so grateful to you too, Lucy Irvine, for stepping in and taking up the huge task of doing the same, and steering me so gracefully onwards.

Like a founding rock of all my books, Pippa Curnick: you came up with the cover illustration for this book like an utter ninja – I had no idea it was coming, and before I could utter 'I wonder what it might look like', there it was and is! Am so thrilled our bookish adventures together continue to go on.

Isobel Lundie: I hardly know what to say . . . You have brought the people I love best to life for me in a way that will have my innards forever smiling. I hope you know how much your care and brilliance means to us, and that you accept my eternal thanks for every second invested in illustrating this book. Yes: I DO need a whole Lundie gallery to myself to hang each portrait up in. And no, of course I will not be staring at them for All Time (lie). Thank you for being such a huge part of the creation of this book baby.

To the sparks of hope and light who go on spreading kindness and justice in revolutionary ways and who I got to mention in this book – Yasmin Ishaq, Caroline Cottet, Charlie Chappers, Jed Tinsley, Ruhi Loren Akhtar, Lorraine Tabone, Dan Atkins, Henrietta MacEwan, Marissa Begonia and Karen Ingala-Smith – thank you, thank you, thank you . . . For being a part of it all – 'it' being the global movement to aid any soul in need, led by hearts who seek no limelight or thanks, and who balance out the world's wrongs with so much that is good, true and humane. It is the absolute honour of my life to know and love each of you as I do, and I cannot imagine a world without you in it, doing what you do to help others each and every day. The same goes for you, Mum and Zak and every dear heart (friends, Trustees, volunteers) who collectively work to keep my worlds at Making Herstory and O's Refugee Aid Team – and through them, so many others – going.

And finally, to The One who continues to gift amal (hope) and noor (light) at every turn, even when all seems to turn too dark to bear: thank you for being, gifting and showing me rays of both these blessings so endlessly and so beautifully, wherever it is I dare look.